Innovation Finance and Technology Transfer

Offering proof-of-concept (POC) to inventors is often a difficult task for most technology transfer office (TTOs). Through an in-depth analysis of 15 years of intellectual property (IP) portfolio management by Oxford University Innovation (OUI), this book identifies the salient aspects of the technology transfer evolution and the role that technology transfer managers (TTMs) and POC play in closing the gap between academia and business.

Innovation Finance and Technology Transfer: Funding proof-of-concept seeks to prove that a well-managed POC fund can achieve positive financial results and that the chances for an IP portfolio management to be "in the money" increases if the TTO is attached to an entrepreneurial university. This work illustrates how innovation based on intellectual property rights, protected and managed by a highly skilled group of TTMs, succeeds in technology transfer. It offers a vademecum to practitioners to follow a step-by-step best practice procedure embraced by the Oxford TTO to manage the POC investment process.

This book provides valuable reading to IP scholars, business school students, social sciences researchers, investment professionals and technology transfer practitioners, as well as those working in innovation think tanks and policy circles.

Andrea Alunni is a world-leading expert in the field of Innovation Finance and Technology Transfer. After working in the City of London as Technology Investment Director, Alunni joined the University of Oxford technology transfer office for a decade to lead the POC investment activity across all research fields.

RIOT!

Routledge Studies in Innovation, Organizations and Technology

Social Entrepreneurship and Social Innovation
Ecosystems for Inclusion in Europe
*Edited by Mario Biggeri, Enrico Testi, Marco Bellucci,
Roel During, Thomas Persson*

Innovation in Brazil
Advancing Development in the 21st Century
*Edited by Elisabeth Reynolds, Ben Ross Schneider and
Ezequiel Zylberberg*

Strategic Renewal
Core Concepts, Antecedents, and Micro Foundations
*Edited by Aybars Tuncdogan, Adam Lindgreen, Henk Volberda,
and Frans van den Bosch*

Service Innovation
Esam Mustafa

Innovation Finance and Technology Transfer
Funding Proof-of-Concept
Andrea Alunni

For more information about the series, please visit www.routledge.com/
Routledge-Studies-in-Innovation-Organizations-and-Technology/book-
series/RIOT

Innovation Finance and Technology Transfer

Funding Proof-of-Concept

Andrea Alunni

Routledge
Taylor & Francis Group

LONDON AND NEW YORK

First published 2019
by Routledge
2 Park Square, Milton Park, Abingdon, Oxon OX14 4RN

and by Routledge
52 Vanderbilt Avenue, New York, NY 10017

Routledge is an imprint of the Taylor & Francis Group, an informa business

British Library Cataloguing-in-Publication Data
A catalogue record for this book is available from the British Library

Library of Congress Cataloging-in-Publication Data
A catalog record has been requested for this book

ISBN: 978-0-367-23210-8 (hbk)
ISBN: 978-0-429-27877-8 (ebk)

Typeset in Times New Roman
by codeMantra

I would like to thank all those who have helped me make this study a reality. I especially wish to express my sincere gratitude to my colleagues Ms Zoe Reich, Ms Linda Naylor and Mr Tom Hockaday. We worked together for almost a decade and without their effective support and mutual learning, I would have been unable to complete this project. I am grateful to them.

Contents

List of illustrations   viii

Introduction   1

1   Technology transfer: a world-class process   7

2   Technology transfer support services: the case of Oxford   22

3   POC funding by the University of Oxford TTO   35

4   POC investment portfolio analysis   50

Conclusions   63

Recommendations   68

References   71
Index   77

Illustrations

Figures

2.1	Standard support services made accessible for IP commercialisation at world-class universities	23
2.2	POC funding value creation in the technology transfer process	28
3.1	The crucial role of POC in the investment process	36
3.2	Impact of POC in the innovation process	37
3.3	POC funding application process	40
3.4	POC investment types offered by OUI	41
3.5	POC funding application guiding questions	42
3.6	Summary of the Advisory Board Evaluation process	44
3.7	Cumulative value of successful POC application	45
4.1	Percentage of POC applications approved, declined or lapsed and number of approvals according to department/field	52
4.2	Idea cloud of a UCSF project	53
4.3	Percentage of POC idea clouds yielding different bands of income	54
4.4	Income density curves for UCSF and non-UCSF idea clouds	55
4.5	Distributions of the number of projects in UCSF and non-UCSF idea clouds	55
4.6	The UCSF annual amount of monies invested by the POC fund over 15 years	59

Tables

1.1	Results obtained from the 2000 AUTM survey	10
4.1	USCF portfolio investment activity (1999–2015)	58
4.2	Annual breakdown of the 157 POC projects awarded	60

Introduction

"If a picture is worth a thousand words, then a prototype is worth a thousand pictures" (Knapp, Zeratsky, & Kowitz, 2016, p. 5). Making the decision to pursue a business idea, is the point at which an inventor meets reality, that is, one can describe the idea to family, friends and potential customers; but if one cannot see it, feel it or really imagine it, no one is going to gain valuable advice and feedback. This is why proof-of-concept (POC [or prototyping and/or exemplification]) is so important in technology transfer. As Upton (2010) sees it, by creating a prototype, it is possible to sit down with a real version of the product and determine which aspects are worthwhile and which parts need to be revised or discarded. The same happens in the experimental process of prototyping a scientific idea. Through prototyping, it may be possible to (i) find omissions that on paper were not noticeable; (ii) get a glimpse of the production process and see if any steps can be changed, combined or even removed to keep the cost of the actual production to a minimum; (iii) see if there are any problems with the POC project design by holding an actual working model; and (iv) assess if a product is sufficiently new or unique for patenting to be considered.

By having a working prototype, it is much easier to see what design aspects may be patentable and/or how the original idea, based on actual experiments, can be changed before production begins (Roy & Group, 1993; Buxton, 2010). For Robbio (2017), prototyping denotes taking a sound scientific idea through to implementation via a crucial POC experiment aimed at providing the intellectual property (IP) with scalability and competitive advantage. From the technology transfer point of view, it could also be argued that POC helps to shape the IP pipeline for future investments by building a negotiating strategic advantage from testing, prototyping and exemplifying the IP to extract value from it before it becomes obsolete (Handler & Maizlish, 2005).

The POC therefore increases technology transfer office (TTO) chances of a larger percentage of the income stream from the commercialisation of innovations so that it can fulfil some main tech-transfer goals, that is, return on investment, job creation, start-up creation, IP licensing and improving reputation at all levels in its own tech-transfer process.

Why is it so difficult for inventors to secure POC?

Offering POC to inventors is often a difficult task for most TTOs. The problem is twofold; on the one hand, POC is at too early a stage to attract private sector-led funding. On the other hand, in the absence of POC, the already high percentage of scientific ideas that never reach the market (or turn into innovative products or services) would increase, subsequently depriving society of innovation.

I posit that POC funding benefits should be perceived beyond the immediate direct returns to universities, as its potential is inherent in the very purpose of POC funding. Moreover, in the longer term, it may well be able to generate opportunities for seed investment in start-ups and, ultimately, venture capitalists (VC) equity investment.

This work concerns POC in tech-transfer, for which funding is normally offered by most advanced TTOs attached to entrepreneurial universities. Here, I would like to highlight that although relatively small sums are needed to carry out crucial experiments (prototyping), yet it helps recognise that the main challenges posed by this process are in the setting where the great majority of ideas never make it to the marketplace, the valley of death.

Besides, in this process of translating innovations into viable products and services, arguments for university participation in a POC fund need to look beyond generating value from tech-transfer per se, as the potential benefits will also include follow-up grants, industry-sponsored research, an enhanced reputation and a broader educational experience through working relationships with start-ups and SMEs. This is why effective POC deployment by entrepreneurial universities depends on high-standard skills to support the process and achieve the financial sustainability of the POC fund, that is, attaining proceeds from outstanding POC portfolio management to keep funding eligible IPs experiments.

It will later be shown how the professional competences needed for a well-functioning POC fund are very much in line with the "soft skills" required for a successful tech-transfer manager profile, which includes knowledge of the environment to identify the right projects, creation of dedicated teams to engage in productive collaboration – and the correct timing for doing so; high-quality intercultural skills to negotiate between academia and the business world so as to foster the mutual trust which is essential to efficient working relationships; and the ability to manage expectations so that means can be matched to ends (Rousseau, Sitkin, Burt, & Camerer, 1998). Equally important, project leaders need a clear overall vision of end-goals, as well as "hard skills" that equip them with sufficient knowledge and authority to discuss and negotiate shareholder expectations and manage conflicts of interest. The POC fund itself and its staff should therefore be similar in scale to a business unit for fast and efficient networking, team building and potential co-investment with SMEs, which combination is instrumental to bridge the gap of early-stage funding.

In this book, I assume that a well-structured TTO can achieve positive financial results from POC funding in the medium to long term and that the chances for its portfolio management to be "in the money" increase if the TTO is attached to an entrepreneurial university.

One of the reasons for supporting this idea is that in perfect financial market conditions, VCs do not see tangible investment opportunity in POC because they tend to have a relatively short investment time horizon, which decreases private-led investment interest in POC. This differs from the long-term investment commitment that TTOs embrace as a fundamental requirement to help universities gain economic benefit, from patenting and licensing to self-finance research activity. Another reason for the success of TTO is the use of best practices. Frequently, best practices converge among advanced TTOs (such as Oxford, MIT and Harvard) and are often a result of the TTOs' capability to align research commercialisation with the mission of these entrepreneurial universities, that is, to generate income for further research and education and to promote economic growth. Another reason is that the financially successful TTOs avoid promoting an IP portfolio that is not developed adequately; in order to plug this gap, they deploy POC funding as a key mechanism not to start IP commercialisation too early, a factor which normally reduces the chances of achieving full positive financial results.

I hope that through this reading you will be able to recognise that, although early-stage financing is always going to be hard to raise when inventions have not even reached the POC stage, POC funding can be used as a key mechanism to succeed in helping universities to commercialise their scientific research. To demonstrate this, I analysed in detail the results of 15 years of POC funding at OUI (the TTO attached to the University of Oxford) and considered POC funding implications based on the two definitions: success in terms of revenues and success in terms of number of connections between POC projects.

Through this quantitative analysis, it has been possible to measure OUI financial success and the significance of its POC funding in advancing IPs to market in technology transfer and how its translational effect has been a determinant in enabling the OUI portfolio management to be "in the money" in the medium-long run. In particular, it has allowed to (i) identify the salient aspects of the technology transfer evolution, with particular emphasis on the role that TTOs play in closing the gap between academia and business; (ii) illustrate how POC plays a central role in generating a compelling investment pipeline for business angels, seed investors and VCs; and (iii) show how a successful TTO in 15 years of POC investment achieved the cumulative financial result that has led it being "in the money" where others have failed.

This work also holds a comprehensive review of existing literature related to the technology transfer process (in all phases, from disclosure of new ideas, IP protection, POC funding deployment to start-up formation) and its TTOs' working mechanisms to identify best practices (policies and procedures), which are of paramount importance to deploying and managing POC funding successfully.

The content of this book is organised in four different chapters: the first one provides an overview of the salient aspects of the technology transfer evolution, with particular emphasis on that from university to society. It also identifies the missing links between research and industry, highlighting the role that TTOs play in closing this gap, and the drivers of the tech-transfer as an advanced process. This first chapter also elucidates reasons as to why the entire tech-transfer process centres on the "human factor", and it advances the idea that, beyond pay at full market rate and excellent working conditions, job satisfaction can be a powerful motivator for this rare and highly qualified category of professionals (or technology transfer managers, TTMs).

The second chapter shows how key stages (the dots) of the technology transfer process connect and explain how POC plays a central role in generating a compelling investment pipeline for business angels, seed investors and VCs. It also describes the services that support the IP portfolio management in prominent TTOs and illustrates how POC develops as a key mechanism for successful research commercialisation within prominent entrepreneurial universities.

The third chapter considers the background in which the POC funding mechanism of the University of Oxford University Challenge Seed Fund (UCSF) was created and examines in detail key operational steps that OUI uses/adopts to successfully deploy and monitor its UCSF POC funding. The steps include POC proposals pre-screening, POC project design, functioning of the Investment Advisory Committee, and monitoring and initial analysis of prospect market. The chapter also touches upon commercialisation (licensing and spin-out) and emphasises how at OUI, this normally comes after a careful consideration of whether or not it is too early to engage with the market. In particular, this consideration is necessary to achieve a twofold advantage from POC funding: first, to increase the chances that a larger percentage of the income stream from IP commercialisation is secured by the University TTO; and second, to negotiate strategic advantage built from testing, prototyping and exemplification in order to timely extract value from IP before it becomes obsolete.

The fourth chapter presents the results of the quantitative analysis carried out to measure the translational effect that POC generated in 15 years of UCSF POC portfolio management by OUI. The analysis allowed measuring of the financial success achieved by OUI in deploying POC funding between 2000 and 2016, based on data available from published sources. It also validated the operative procedures and best practices observed to test, prototype and/or exemplify the technology as a way of accelerating IPs' commercialisation out of the university and into the marketplace. It shows how relatively small POC investments produced a translational effect that helped OUI build over time a sound POC pipeline that successfully progressed new technologies to early adopters and later-stage traditional investors.

This book takes into consideration only projects with IP at the core. Those are the target of POC investment. It does not focus on TTO performance, given the fact that a good TTO performance does not necessarily secure positive financial results for a POC fund. The book makes specific reference to financial elements that are important to attract private sector-led funding, but does not consider fund-raising techniques for the POC fund, as this would entail a separate analysis.

I have worked in technology transfer for more than a decade, seen first-hand how different TTOs deal with POC activity and tracked TTOs' performance, best practices and POC funding impact. I have relied on my personal experience to carry out this work with selected, representative and reliable data, appropriate methodology and no bias assumptions.

It is anticipated that the chapters of this book contain new and useful guidance to private and public bodies interested in developing, managing and investing in a portfolio of intellectual property rights (IPRs) and to those interested in developing new solutions from scientific ideas for a sustainable development in the light of current global unprecedented technological changes. It will be of particular relevance to those interested in best practices adopted by prominent TTOs to generate positive financial results in an unconventional time-frame to benefit investors, research and the innovation process which, in turn, favours jobs and wealth creation for society as a whole. It is also expected that this reading will be of help to TTO managers and early-stage technology investors when deploying POC funding or looking for POC investment opportunities, respectively, by providing them with a clear picture of how a world-class TTO selects and manages POC project portfolio successfully.

I also hope that the conclusions resulting from this work will help public- and private-led sceptical investors to see the benefits of investing in early-stage technologies and to approach this area with more attention in order to identify interesting funding opportunities at the initial IP commercialisation stages which have been opened up by POC.

1 Technology transfer

A world-class process

This chapter provides an overview of the salient aspects of the technology transfer evolution, with particular emphasis on that from university to society. It also identifies the missing links between research and industry (human factor and impact finance), highlighting the role that TTOs play in closing this gap, and the drivers of the tech-transfer as an advanced process. It also elucidates reasons as to why the entire tech-transfer process centres on the "human factor", and advances the idea that job satisfaction can be a powerful motivator for this rare and highly qualified category of professionals (or TTMs), other than being in receipt of pay at full market rate and outstanding working conditions.

Technology transfer is defined by Cooksey "as the process to assist the successful transformation of good research into good business" (as cited in Isis Innovation Report 2010). This is supported by Roessner (2000) who also takes into account tech-transfer as "the formal and informal movement of know-how, skills, technical knowledge or technology from one organizational setting to another" (p. 23). He points out that because the process often faces unfavourable economic incentives and an inadequate supply of complementary services to translate new ideas into technological and economically viable innovations, its coordination among various stakeholders is a challenge. The technology transfer process, he continues, also requires access to a number of informational, financial and human resources. Both authors correctly identify the role of tech-transfer in closing the gap between research and business and the need for the process, once in place, to align stakeholders in a common mission and vision, and its implementation with institutional determination to embrace the draconian task of supporting researchers/inventors to move a protected idea (IP) successfully to the market (Roessner, 2000; Isis Innovation Report, 2010).

Technology transfer has become central in recent university evolution and has gained remarkable importance in terms of both the challenges and opportunities it presents to the life-long effort of individual inventors in finding suitable solutions to old and new problems for the progress of societies. Technology transfer is a new and complex process that works in an unconventional timeframe and at a high level of uncertainty. A successful technology transfer process requires strong research to generate a sound IP portfolio, a dedicated TTO as a meeting point of science and business, a team of highly skilled TTMs who understand the languages of science and business, and a surrounding entrepreneurial ecosystem capable of absorbing innovation and providing ancillary services. Additionally, to make this business viable, it is necessary that the resources involved are available at the right level and are managed efficiently.

In a historical note, Campinos (2018), on the occasion of the first EUIPO workshop, aptly pointed out that technology transfer is as old as human invention, since it has fuelled human development and innovation across the globe through the millennia, from the Bronze Age to the present. Over time, however, the concept has changed to become a political and corporate mantra, often surrounded by analytical ambiguities that affect research and theory (Bozeman, 2000).

For many centuries, after the first patent legislation in the Italian city of Venice in 1474 (Penrose & Zamora, 1974), European universities and those in the United States were not involved in bringing new inventions to society. Discoveries made by scientists through publicly funded universities became the property of the governments that provided the money, and consequently, those discoveries were published in the scientific literature rather than patented (Geuna & Nesta, 2006).

In the context of innovation theory and practice, the emergence of technology transfer as an explicit concept has been attributed to Vannevar Bush, a political advisor to US President Roosevelt, for US postwar economic recovery (as cited in Science: The Endless Frontier, 1945), for indicating clear linkages between public investment in research & development (R&D) and the commercialisation of technology. As emphasised by the former MIT President Jerome Wiesner (1979), thanks to Bush's position, public investment in R&D continues and many of the most important US discoveries have since emerged. His recommendation to the US government, therefore, made it possible for important experiments undertaken (with very different purposes in mind) to continue and highly useful discoveries to result from certain elements of the research undertakings in basic science.

Publicly funded universities versus scientific inventions management

In the aftermath of the Second World War (WWII), there were very few universities in the USA that were engaged in the patenting and licensing of inventions, for two main reasons: first, most universities viewed this as an activity which diverted faculty attention from teaching and research; and, second, the problem of securing funding for research beyond the Federal Government persisted because there was no legislation to deal with the matter of patent licensing arising from public funding (Etzkowitz, Webster, Gebhardt, & Terra, 2000).

At the same time in Europe, legislation was also mostly lacking, and with the exception of Germany, in general, there was little interest across Europe in commercialising publicly funded research (Harhoff & Hoisl, 2007). Germany's Employees' Inventions Act of 1957, which gave more autonomy to academic inventors, made Germany one of the few countries in which the monetary compensation for inventors is not only determined by negotiations between employer and employee-inventor, but also by relatively precise legal provisions.

Due to this lack of legislation, for a long time, industry and academia operated in vastly different spheres, and even where pathways from public invention to private commercialisation existed (i.e. where private companies could enter into institutional patent agreements with universities), it was an uneasy process with rules varying between universities and government agencies.

Technology transfer evolution – from university to society

The Bayh Dole Act (also referred to as Public Law 96–517), enacted in the USA in 1980, was the historical event that propelled the current evolution of tech-transfer from universities to society, and it is tightly linked to the evolution of licensing in the USA, particularly the licensing of research by universities. From here onwards, the focus will be on this specific type of licensing.

The Bayh-Dole Act was therefore born to facilitate research spin-out by universities and to encourage economic benefit from patenting and licensing of university research results. The law implied that Federal Government research funding (which is about 65% of all research funding for US universities) could be reduced if such a technology transfer function was not established via the Technology Licensing Office (TLO).

Measuring the intent of the Act on technology transfer in the USA and beyond

Due to the lack of legislation before the Act, up until 1980 in the USA, only 30,000 patents accrued through federally funded research; around 1,200 were licensed, and even fewer had made it to the market. Fortunately, in the USA, an association of University Licensing Professionals, the Society of University Patent Administrators (SUPA), formed in 1974, was already in place; it was then renamed Association of University Technology Managers (AUTM) in 1989, which made it possible to bring about a convergence on best practices throughout the entire country through meetings, courses and publications based on annual surveys of patenting and licensing results which have emerged since its foundation. The intent of the Act was measured by an AUTM survey to mark the new millennium (Roessner, Bond, Okubo, & Planting, 2013). The survey results display, by almost any measure, the great economic growth that patenting and licensing has been yielding from university research in the USA up to the year 2000.

Table 1.1 summarises the results obtained from the 2000 AUTM survey.

After this consolidated success, the trends in the US Federal Government to encourage technology transfer from university to society included further legislations and policies to encourage strong technology transfer as an emerging profession within the US universities. They include (i) the creation of the Advanced Technology Program (ATP) and STTR (SBIR extension to include universities) Programs to encourage university/industry collaboration; (ii) the government's large investments in support of the federal laboratory system (600 laboratories, 100,000 scientists, $25 billion) enabling the passing of the 1986 Fed Lab T/T Act, which required royalty sharing with inventors and also encouraged Cooperative Research Development Agreements (or CRADAs) to promote industry/laboratory collaborations; and

Table 1.1 Results obtained from the 2000 AUTM survey

2000 AUTM survey
$1,260 million in royalties
$60 billion in licensed products sales
400,000 new jobs
13,032 new invention disclosures
6,375 new patent filings
4,362 new licenses (12% to start-up companies)

(iii) tax policies with regard to stock options and capital gain rates have also encouraged university/industry collaboration (Brint, 2005).

Similar initiatives were subsequently encouraged by the UK government, and, following the issue of the UK report "White Paper on the United Kingdom's Competitiveness" in 1998, many policy initiatives and government funding streams were established to stimulate cooperation between the researchers in universities and the country's industrial entrepreneurs. This cooperation significantly changed the way universities in the UK organise their technology transfer activities (Keay, 2007). Several prominent UK universities created separate companies to commercialise IP, especially innovations that were thought to have the potential to serve as foundations for spin-out companies (university companies or UNICOs). Nonetheless, the majority of universities also have internal TTOs that collaborate closely with the sponsored-research office and with the UNICOs to develop industry relationships. Further growth and development of TTOs have been stimulated more recently by direct government funding to universities for a third-stream activity via the Higher Education Innovation Fund (HEIF) in England and Wales and the Scottish Executive Expertise, Knowledge, and Innovation Transfer Programme (SEEKIT). Initially, HEIF financial support was awarded to institutions through competitive solicitation. Today, the government distributes HEIF funds directly to universities through a formula funding process which is based upon numerous criteria, including, but not limited to, institutional research capacity (quantity and quality) and TTO performance measures.

After almost four decades of proactive technology transfer practice in North America, and throughout the world, the licensing debate now focuses more on what is the best model of IP ownership for academic institutions and other public research organisations in the future. According to Young et al. (2007), in the USA, for example, the institution-owned model (except for the University of Wisconsin) prevails, while in Canada, the inventor-owned model is more popular in many institutions. Several countries in various parts of the world have also moved recently to the institution-owned model (Japan, Germany and the United Kingdom, for example). However, it seems that the inventor-owned model and the institution-owned model both have positive and negative attributes.

How technology transfer keeps evolving from university to society?

By definition, technology transfer is the process by which new innovations flow from the basic research bench to commercial entities and then to public use (Van Norman & Eisenkot, 2017). In order to succeed in this endeavour, research institutions clearly need to boost their capacities for transforming the ideas that stem from research into new and innovative technological applications that benefit society as a whole. A vibrant culture of technology and innovation is required to drive economic success sustained by research and to attract the best and most creative inventors, entrepreneurs, researchers, students and academics of excellence to work together. In order to thrive in innovation, universities need to be equally ambitious both in technology transfer and in achieving excellence in teaching and research. This means placing much greater emphasis on extracting value from IP.

Closing the gap between research and industry – the missing links

Today, the main challenge in the complex process of translating innovations into viable products/services is that the great majority of ideas, whether protected or not, never make it to the marketplace. The reasons for this are as complex and varied as the tech-transfer process itself; yet, the missing links essentially relate to gaps in two areas: the human factor, discussed in this chapter (see "Technology transfer is a people's business"), and impact funding for the early stages of POC, prototyping and demonstration – addressed later in Chapter 2.

Technology transfer involves an advanced process where TTOs are crucial in harnessing the potential of consolidating research and industry networks to develop technology transfer activities based on innovation-friendly procedures, and in promoting appropriate funding mechanisms to support each different stage of the process.

A world-class university TTO is an entrepreneurial office with a dedicated team aiming to establish new spin-out ventures or create licensing agreements based on protected IP and with a university funding mechanisms devoted to strengthen the technology transfer process.

TTOs' requirements to consolidate research and industry networks

To support the university in the effort of consolidating research and industry networks, TTOs' fundamental requirements are (1) excellency in managing the quality and quantity of research generated within the university, (2) capability to align research commercialisation with the institution's mission and (3) being adept at making a long-term commitment to the required institutional changes and to invest adequately in resources and people. Here, each requirement is considered in detail.

Managing the quality and quantity of research generated within the university

The most compelling forces that determine a university TTO's characteristics and performance are the volume of research activity within the institution and the quality of the research results (Siegel, Waldman, Atwater, & Link, 2003). This is why world-class universities tend to make sure that all new inventions they develop are disclosed to their own TTO, as it will then coordinate the efforts of the inventors, patent attorneys and commercial partners throughout the technology transfer/commercialisation process.

For universities to secure research excellence, there is a need to stimulate outstanding scientists to codify their tacit knowledge into valuable patents, while the disclosure of ideas (from professors, researchers and students) is encouraged to flow from their different research departments, colleges and/or institutes to the university's own TTO, in order to build up an IP portfolio to manage and create technology transfer opportunities. Sourcing innovative ideas from academic research often entails observations and experiments during research activities, which, in turn, may lead to discoveries and inventions. An invention is any useful process, machine, composition of matter or any new or useful improvement of the same. Often, multiple researchers may have contributed to the invention.

Academic excellence is therefore a powerful source of innovation, and this excellence is often measured by the quantity and quality of publications. This principle has been enriched over time, when one also considers that universities have a mission to ensure that their discoveries, inventions and new science applications lead to useful products and services for the public, and that a timely emphasis on extracting relevant value from IP is necessary before it becomes obsolete (Cook, 2007).

Aligning research commercialisation with university mission

The success of technology transfer depends, as for any deal, on each party finding a benefit in the transaction (IPIC, 2017). The need to share the benefits is the reason why IP is fundamental to technology transfer. Whatever the route followed for technology transfer, the rules and agreements – who owns the IP or who can use the IP, and who pays what to whom regarding the IP – form the basis of any deal to ensure that each party benefits (Geuna & Nesta, 2006). However, there is a substantial difference between the approaches used to commercialise research depending on its source of creation. Academia, for example, tends to encourage the free exchange of ideas, while researchers in the private sector will normally pursue experiments that are part of a larger corporate goal driven by market needs.

The private sector normally shares its own work with fellow researchers in the company; however, their efforts are usually kept secret from the general public because of the potential monetary value of the inventions the researchers generate. Secrecy is, of course, in contrast with the mission of universities, although it includes commercialisation of its research results for the public good when it generates income for further research, education and promotion of economic growth (Sapsalis, de la Potterie, & Navon, 2006).

Commercial approaches to research commercialisation can also vary significantly among countries. A comparative study by Carayannis, Cherepovitsyn, and Ilinova (2016) between Russian and US tech-transfer models, for example, found that the US universities lead in technology commercialisation, while Russians tend to lag far behind because of the lack of a standard process for administration, research and business activity that promotes innovation and entrepreneurship.

Objectives for research commercialisation

World-class universities align their mission and objectives with their own TTOs to commercialise their own research and comply with the third mission (education being the first, and research the second). Most TTO's mission focuses upon three primary objectives: services to the academics, economic development and income to the university. That is,

Services to the academics: are provided to the university researchers in exchange for a percentage of the income from successful commercialization of the IP. This commercialization revenue partially subsidizes the TTO office. Researcher satisfaction is typically high because all disclosures receive TTO attention and a dedicated manager (Wheaton, 2006).

Economic development: is inspired by the university goal to create jobs and economic growth through the establishment of spin-out companies and through licensing to local companies. According to Rothaermel and Thursby (2005) research centers and university institutions are indisputably the most important factor in incubating high-tech industries, i.e. 29 of the top 30 high-tech clusters in the United States were home to a comprehensive research university.

Income: the TTO commercialization objective focuses on earning revenues from the transfer of new technologies to companies by being very selective in identifying innovations with the highest potential. This activity over time has led to overall researcher satisfaction, which is favourable as most universities have a strong researcher-service orientation. Institutions with higher income levels from licensing are typically teaching/research centres of excellence where the chance of an outstanding commercial success is more realistic. Naturally, TTOs do not focus on a single mission, but combine their vision in ways that best satisfy their own constituents and stakeholders.

Coping with long-term commitment to invest adequately in resources and people

The university's willingness to make a long-term commitment to the TTO is fundamental. This aspect has been the greatest predictor of success in terms of its cumulative results and performance measures. For instance, as new disclosures, patent applications and licence agreements are added cumulatively each year to the TTO's portfolio, the chances that a fraction of these will eventually generate returns continue to increase.

Technology transfer entails an unconventional timeframe for traditional investment. Technology transfer practitioners suggest that it typically takes five or more years for a technology that is licensed to an industry partner to result in a marketable product. Thus, according to these practitioners, TTOs require seven to ten years to become successful, regardless of how one chooses to measure success (Swamidass & Vulasa, 2009). Institutions should therefore expect similar experiences and be prepared to subsidise the office for many years (more than a two- or three-year financial obligation), in order to allow time to build a team of highly skilled TTMs who understand the languages of science and business, and consolidate a surrounding entrepreneurial ecosystem capable of absorbing innovation and of providing ancillary services.

Technology transfer is a people's business

Technology transfer is all about people, from the inventor of an idea through to the end-customer once the idea has reached the market.

Much innovation happens randomly, with no particular focus on its end-purposes; therefore, it is essential to consider what one wants to achieve by translating innovations into marketable products and services.

Because innovation and bringing innovations to the market are primarily about people, there is no single model that can fit every situation. Universities and research labs interact with businesses in many different ways, from collaborative research to IP licensing, conferences, publications and graduate recruitment. However, TTOs attached to universities are the ones specialised in facilitating these interactions. The entire tech-transfer process centres on the "human factor", which is therefore crucial to the mediation that needs to take place between the many people from widely differing professional and cultural backgrounds who all have a role to play in the various stages of moving the technology transfer process forward, up to and including the end-customer.

In order to build closer ties to industry and facilitate the commercialisation of research, it is essential for a TTO to recruit, reward and retain high-quality TTMs. TTO staff need to be talented, highly motivated but also motivational, highly trained and knowledgeable in widely differing and rapidly evolving fields of activity, and also be able to effectively mediate between science and business. They are the people who help all the parties reach agreement and conclude transactions in the tech-transfer process. And it is when those transactions happen that innovation happens.

Technology transfer managers – an emerging profession

As an emerging professional category to boost innovation, universities need specific information and management skills to set up tech-transfer partnerships; inventors need a "safe place" in which to discuss the conditions, end-purposes and costs of disclosing their ideas; investors need understanding and reassurance as to the security, yields and purposes of their investments; companies – especially small and medium-sized enterprises (SMEs) whose flexibility and entrepreneurial spirit is crucial to developing ideas for the market – need guidance and pointers to potential R&D partnerships as well as a thorough understanding of the potential customers for their products.

Many of the issues revolve around understanding and accepting risks, and this implies bright people at the negotiating interfaces whose profile encompasses not only a working knowledge of IP processes and pitfalls, but also experience and understanding of widely diverse professional areas and cultures, the ability to "speak the language" of both academia and business, and a wide range of contact networks, all combined with what is generally referred to as "people skills".

Clearly, what is outlined here is an emerging, but as yet hazy, profession of TTMs. Among the several questions that arise around this emerging profession are: What qualifications should be devised for these new professionals? How would their continuing training be ensured in order to allow them to keep up with the rapidly evolving demands of technology transfer?

At present, tech-transfer agencies are diversely fragmented within the different segments in the tech-transfer process, and no qualifications or standards exist for the role of TTMs dedicated to helping innovations make the important leap to the market. The technology transfer role differs according to the market, but experience in end-to-end product development and launch is fundamental. This includes familiarity with regulatory aspects, including IP. A scientific background is a plus, but also experience in economics and finance, especially in modelling that can be applied to the successive business cycles involved in the tech-transfer process.

Not only is the role of a TTM exceptionally demanding in terms of skills and responsibilities, but it will also vary with different markets, different "ecosystems" and different levels of innovation. A good TTM will need to understand and distinguish different levels of innovation and their social, economic and financial impacts. The first level is "sustaining" innovation, where the goal is to replace old with new and better products so that the key question for a TTM is, "can this innovation prolong existing revenue growth?" The skills required are therefore relatively straightforward. The second level is "efficiency-driven" innovation, which essentially seeks to produce more with less. The key question here is, "does this innovation improve profit margins?" The third level is "market-creating" innovation, where the job of a TTM is far more complex. The key question is, "does the innovation resolve a large and complex issue better than existing solutions?" These are transformational innovations, which characteristically generate higher risks, but also have a greater impact.

Moreover, the TTM role is necessarily cross-functional: a TTM needs to be "conversant" rather than "expert" in different fields. However, not only do they need to "speak the language" of different fields, but they also have to do so with sufficient authority, for example, to select and reject projects, manage conflicts of interest, and judge the best timing of actions and interactions with the different players. This brings in the question of accountability for the project outcome: this is generally attributed to the marketing role, but some TTM accountability is essential, because the TTM will be involved in the process from beginning to end. In the fast-moving sector of technological innovation, this implies a continuous on-the-job learning process for TTMs.

What kind of training should this emerging profession envisage?

Given the very demanding and diversified role of a TTM, what kind of training should be envisaged for this emerging profession, and in what environment? In the USA, there is an association of University Licensing Professionals, the SUPA, formed in 1974 and then renamed Association of University Technology Managers (AUTM) in 1989, that makes it possible to bring about a convergence on best practices throughout the entire country through meetings, courses and publications based on annual surveys of patenting and licensing results (Roessner et al., 2013). While in Europe, for example, there already exists a joint doctorate in IP under a Horizon 2020 grant (Borrell-Damian et al., 2010), in order to promote research on the role of IP in innovation, to improve support to investors and entrepreneurs in managing the life cycle of IP-intensive assets and to strengthen the process of translating innovation into commercially viable products, which is where the benefits lie for industry and society as a whole.

The very rapidly evolving and very diverse landscape of innovation and tech-transfer suggests that formal training should include a strong apprenticeship component encompassing the different phases and interactions in a variety of situations (Siegel & Phan, 2005). The experience of those currently involved in TTM, in every part of the world, strongly suggests that the crucial needs are industrial or engineering experience, some specialisation in a given field (water, environment, agro-biotech, etc.) and on-the-job learning, whether in a start-up, SME or larger company.

In the current context, it is becoming more important that the skills of the job should be codified through formal qualifications and certification (Walshok & Shapiro, 2014). This would help to attract the necessary talent in addition to bringing a measure of standardisation into the training offered. In designing training, attracting people to the TTM role should be investigated from the point of view of potential recruits: the required versatile profile points to expectations of fluidity between different areas in which they exercise their skills and contribute to the whole process, for example, from lab to doctorate to law firm to start-up. An initial professional qualification involving internships would be well suited to the operational requirements of the TTM role by potentially laying the foundations for alliance-based relationships through teamwork.

Apprenticeship-based learning with a mix of classroom, business and IP training would provide a powerful incentive for talented young people to engage in tech-transfer; however, this raises the question of appropriate training organisations. Business school training does not generally provide students with opportunities to work with entrepreneurs: business schools compete with each other for future students and donors, and are ranked on metrics that give particular weight to starting salaries, thus attracting students to work in finance and large corporations rather than with SMEs and entrepreneurs that create value throughout the economic fabric of a society. This is especially problematic when students start looking for work with a large student loan to pay off. The attraction will also vary with environment, location and the working conditions offered.

At present, internships offer the best chance of securing the engagement of talented young people, who, in some cases, reach an "associate" status supporting senior officers, on the lines of law firms (Hazelkorn, 2009). The question of fluidity raises the problem of where the TTMs should be based. In other words, for whom is the TTM working? At present, the majority work for the university attached TTOs; however, given that the new generation of accelerators is increasingly working as "match-makers" with the corporate sector, TTMs working for these structures could be increasingly relevant.

How to motivate and reward world-class TTMs?

TTM professionals can be rewarded based on their:

- financial success. They may be paid a performance-related salary or be given a financial share in a successful deal
- community-building success. Being part of a team engaged in a worthwhile activity is its own reward
- civic or humanitarian contribution. Contributing to a national or local economy is a satisfying accomplishment, and the most appropriate basis for reward will vary from situation to situation.

In some cases, there may be limitations on the kinds of rewards that can be given, as any bonus that a TTM receives may negatively affect relationships with university colleagues. For example, at the University of Oxford, the technology transfer staff (who are not university staff members but are employed by a company owned by the university) work closely with members of the university administration on commercialisation projects. If one such project were to produce a large financial gain for the technology transfer staff but not for the university employees, their relationship would be strained (Cook, 2007).

At the Oxford University TTO, for example, each technology transfer project manager deals with about 40 projects at a time. That is, each manager supports at least 40 individual researchers. If one such project became very successful, both the TTM and the researcher who generated the technology would, of course, be pleased. However, the other researchers in the manager's portfolio may feel that their own projects had not been given appropriate attention, and their relationships with the manager might suffer.

As Cook (2007) observes, probably the most powerful motivator for many TTMs is not financial but intellectual, that is, the pride inherent in associating with creative scientists and collaborating in the creation of new products. It is profoundly rewarding to be the person who brings an invention, whether it is a drug or a software product, from a university researcher's desk to the market. Indeed, it is rewarding to employ one's skills to bring together the academic, financial and commercial communities and make something new happen. Clearly, this sort of intangible motivation only works if the TTO pays its staff at market rate, provides excellent working conditions and recognises that job satisfaction can be a powerful motivator. This seems to recall the "Matthew Effect" suggested by Merton (1968) that conceives ways in which certain psychosocial processes affect the allocation of rewards to scientists for their contributions and how it influences the flow of ideas and findings through the communication networks of science.

In this first chapter, an overview of salient aspects of the technology transfer evolution have been provided, with particular emphasis on definitions from a range of authors and practitioners who highlight the role that TTOs play in closing the gap between academia and business. The fundamental requirements for an advanced TTO to support the university were discussed in details for (1) excellency in managing the quality and quantity of research generated within the university, (2) capability to align research commercialisation with the institution's mission and (3) being adept at making a long-term commitment to the required institutional changes and to invest adequately in resources and people. This chapter has also provided insights into an emerging professional category, the TTMs, a rare and highly qualified group of individuals who support the academic, financial and commercial communities to make something new happen.

Main takeaways include the following: first, the Bayh Dole Act (also referred to as Public Law 96–517), enacted in the USA in 1980, was the historical event that propelled the current evolution of tech-transfer from universities to society; and, second, that the missing links to bridge the gap between research and industry within the technology transfer process essentially relate to human factor (see in this chapter "Technology transfer is a people's business") and impact funding for the early stages of POC, prototyping and demonstration (to be addressed in Chapter 2). The next chapter will also show how key stages of the technology transfer process connect in order to promote innovation.

2 Technology transfer support services

The case of Oxford

The second chapter describes the services that support IP portfolio management in prominent TTOs and, based on the University of Oxford experience, illustrates how POC develops as a key mechanism for successful research commercialisation within prominent entrepreneurial universities. It also shows how key stages (the dots) of the technology transfer process connect to promote innovation, and it explains how the fundamental incompatibility between the instrumental role of POC in advancing scientific ideas to the market and the persistent reluctance of private investors to fund prototypes calls on university mission to fill this gap by generating income from patenting and licensing to self-finance university research and education, and promote economic growth through innovation.

> Technology transfer does not just happen. Transferring knowledge and innovation from a public research organization to the private sector for commercial application and public benefit requires a formal mechanism – a technology transfer office (TTO) – to protect and license intellectual property.
>
> (Young et al., 2007, p. 545)

In order to promote innovation, though, this mechanism should be based on innovation-friendly procedures to support each different stage of the process.

Registering and protecting IP is an essential stepping stone on the way to the market success of an invention. However, according to Maskus (2000), regardless of their potential, many ideas – up to 95% in the USA, for example – never progress beyond the protection or patenting stage, so that the creative efforts and funds invested up to that point are wasted.

The increasingly diversified and rapidly changing landscape of innovation clearly requires a major capacity-building effort to equip technology transfer players with the necessary skills and resources to ensure success. In practice, capacity building needs to encompass not only training and qualifications to shape the right skills, but also workable and accessible mechanisms to fund the crucial but necessarily risky proof-of-concept required to bring ideas beyond the protection or patenting stage to the market.

Technology transfer offices services to support innovation

Advanced TTOs attached to entrepreneurial universities support researchers, inventors and entrepreneurs during the course of starting a new venture based on IP. Figure 2.1 shows the standard support services made accessible for IP commercialisation at world-class universities, and these may vary depending on the TTO's size, policy and procedures.

To identify the foremost common support services offered in tech-transfer, a selection of prominent TTOs in high-income countries was considered regarding the quantity and quality of research they deal with. Following is the list that summarises the top ten common support services offered:

1 Invention disclosure: The written notice of invention to the university TTO is the beginning of the formal technology transfer process. An invention disclosure remains a confidential document,

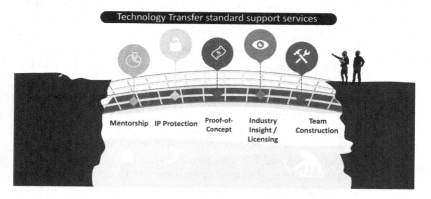

Figure 2.1 Standard support services made accessible for IP commercialisation at world-class universities.

and should fully record an invention so that the options for commercialisation can be evaluated and pursued. An invention disclosure should ideally be submitted before any disclosure of the technology is made outside the university community.

2 Invention assessment: This is the period in which the applicant and the designated TTM review the invention disclosure, conduct patent searches (if applicable) and analyse the market and competitive landscape to determine the invention's commercialisation potential. The evaluation process, which may lead to a broadening or refinement of the invention, will guide TTO strategy on whether to focus on licensing to an existing company or to focus on creating a new business start-up.

3 Idea protection: This is a process in which protection for an invention is pursued to encourage third-party interest in commercialisation. Patent protection, a common legal protection method, begins with the filing of a patent application with the relevant patent office and, when appropriate, foreign patent offices. Once a patent application has been filed, it will require several years and many thousands of euros to obtain patents for the issuing country as well as foreign patents. Other protection options include copyright, trademark and design protection.

4 POC: With active researcher/inventor involvement, TTO staff will consider if the identified IP should apply for POC funding; in order *to verify that its concept/principle has the potential for real-world application*, it will do so by producing a prototype that is designed to determine feasibility, but does not represent deliverables. This step will be treated in-depth in this and the following chapter of this book.

5 IP commercialisation: TTO staff will identify candidate IP companies that have the expertise, resources and business networks to bring the technology to market. This may involve partnering with an existing company or forming a start-up. Active researcher/inventor involvement can dramatically shorten this process.

6 Start-up formation: If creation of a new business start-up has been chosen as the optimal commercialisation path, the TTO's Designated Coordinator of New Ventures will assist in the process of planning, creating and funding the start-up.

7 Licensing to existing business partners: If an appropriate and interested existing business is identified as a potential licensee, TTO licensing specialists will identify mutual interests, goals and plans to fully commercialise the technology through a license agreement.

8 Legal support: A licence agreement is a contract between the university and a third party in which the university's rights to a technology are licensed (without relinquishing ownership) for financial and other benefits. A licence agreement is used with both a new start-up business and with an established company. An option agreement is sometimes used to enable a third party to evaluate the technology for a limited time before licensing.

9 Commercialisation after licensing: The licensee company continues the advancement of the technology, and makes other business investments to develop the product or service. This step may entail further development, regulatory approvals, sales and marketing, support, training and other activities.

10 Licensing revenue distribution: Set portions of the revenues received by the university from licensees are distributed to the inventors, the university and other institutions (in the case of jointly owned inventions) to fund additional research and education and to encourage further participation in the tech-transfer process.

The set-up of the University of Oxford TTO

The University of Oxford established its own TTO in 1988 in response to the growing need of managing the constant flow of patentable idea disclosures originating from the vast research activity carried out in the University of Oxford across all subjects (Isis Innovation Report, 2010). The OUI, formerly named *Isis Innovation*, was created as an external commercial company wholly owned by the university with the mandate of the TTO of the university. This happened a decade before the government issued its 1998 report, "White Paper on the United Kingdom's Competitiveness", to stimulate policy initiatives and government funding streams.

Following the report, several prominent UK universities created separate companies to commercialise IP, in particular innovations that were thought to have potential to serve as foundations for spin-out companies. The subsequent cooperation between the researchers at universities and the country's industrial entrepreneurs in the UK gave the initiative considerable impetus.

An entrepreneurial environment is key to support tech-transfer

Although the extensive research activity carried out in Oxford across all subjects is financed with an annual research budget now close to

£600 million (Isis Innovation Report, 2015), the University TTO depends upon a number of factors, among which the most important is *the entrepreneurial culture of the institution and its entourage* (at national, regional and local levels). This institutional culture is determined by the attitude and degree of support from the university decision makers. At OUI, this has enabled the expansion of its initial technology transfer operations to include activities in support of specific industry partners, creating closer connections to the corporate sector, such as the development of spin-out-company business plans by the university's business school (Said), the creation of university-based technology business incubators (The Startup Incubator and the Foundry), its research and science parks and seed and venture funds. Because of its entrepreneurial culture, the university interconnects with the local innovation ecosystem and relevant institutions through its dedicated TTO to secure a commercialisation path of the IP portfolio.

From the operational point of view, the framework of policies laid out by the university clarifies the role of the researchers, the TTO, the university and the private sector which act in symbiosis within the innovation ecosystem; that is, the policies align the interests of the individuals and institution, building incentives for the researchers to disclose their ideas to the University TTO in order to perform an initial screening and assessment before filing the IP for protection. These incentives are transparently communicated by the university, stating from the outset the proportion of revenue sharing between the university and the inventors. Historically, around 30% of researchers engage in technology transfer at Oxford, contributing to a growing trend towards creating an additional revenue stream for the institution and the individual inventors.

More importantly, any single project at OUI receives not only the support of TTO staff, but also that of entrepreneurs in the local ecosystem willing to help. Selection of local advisors is based on their background in a technical discipline, on their business acumen, on having considerable experience in start-up and early-stage technology ventures, and on holding significant connections to local companies and investment sources. These connections are extremely valuable as they constitute the link between the technologies invented by researchers and the crucial external networks of the private-led sector.

External advisors and VC fund managers work in partnership with representatives from the university TTMs who are responsible for protecting the IP, negotiating and executing the licence agreements and forming new start-ups (Gulbranson & Audretsch, 2008). The TTO also works in coordination with other universities and community-led organisations to coach, offer guidance and identify entrepreneurs and investment capital sources that can help the nascent companies move down the commercialisation path (Cooper, 2014).

POC as a key IP commercialisation mechanism at Oxford

The University of Oxford technology transfer is a step-by-step process that can be conceptualised as a continuous cycle wherein innovative ideas are developed into licensed products that then help fund the next generation of research and innovation. Most of the steps to follow are similar, regardless of whether the company commercialising the technology is a new venture or an established one. They are particularly relevant to entrepreneurs starting a new venture based on Oxford IP. At Oxford, as in most prominent TTOs, the technology transfer process begins with the completion of an invention record by a researcher and then follows the route that will be described in the next paragraphs of this chapter.

A feature that characterises the University of Oxford TTO technology transfer process is the principle of not starting the commercialisation phase too early, in order to avoid promoting an IP portfolio which is not developed adequately. For this reason, the OUI often deploys POC funding as a key IP commercialisation mechanism to plug this gap.

The OUI POC fund team makes advisory services available to all researchers of the University, even if they do not receive funding from the POC fund. The OUI also provides incubation space and required meeting locations for pre-companies to operate before they secure capital and execute the necessary licence agreement. The funding model of the OUI (including its POC fund) has evolved around two essential features: (i) that a percentage of the income stream from IP commercialisation is allocated to the TTO, and (ii) that the OUI has increasingly become financially self-sustaining from this allocation of income and other related income-generating services.

The importance of funding POC in advancing IPs to market

POC funding is vital to trigger a successful tech-transfer process, but it is also the least likely to attract private finance. Academic research is often viewed as being at too early a stage to attract interest from venture investors or from companies (start-ups or SMEs) that would develop it further, while conventional public grant schemes rarely support the POC research needed to exemplify university technologies.

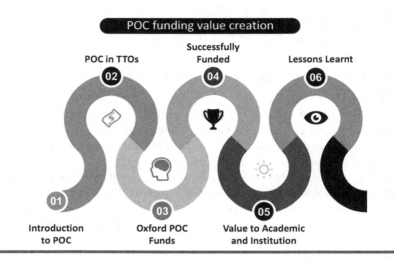

Figure 2.2 POC funding value creation in the technology transfer process.

One of the roles of POC funds at the OUI is therefore to shape the pipeline for future investment from the private-led sector. Figure 2.2 shows the POC funding value creation in the technology transfer process.

Different types of early-stage funds exist – seed funds, angel groups, incubators, early-stage venture capital and so on – but before these are called on, POC funding is essential to prepare the technologies for further investment. As with all aspects of technology transfer, however, the picture and the risks vary with different goals and environments.

At present, worldwide, only some 30 funds focusing on university innovation can be classified as POC funds, with an average investment of £25,000–£50,000, although a £5,000 figure is not unusual, with the top-end at around £100,000 in the UK. In the USA, the SBIR and STTR programmes have been fostering early-stage finance successfully, with funds averaging $1.5–$5 million (National Research Council, 2009a). In Europe, most R&D funding is on a large scale from EU research funds (FPRD, H2020) and the European Council, and hence the need to foster emerging initiatives to bridge the funding gap commensurately with early-stage needs.

Nevertheless, POC to inventors is often a difficult task for most TTOs. The problem is that POC is at too early a stage to attract private sector-led funding; in the absence of POC, the already high percentage of scientific ideas that never reach the market (or turn into innovative products or services) would increase, subsequently depriving society of innovation. As such, one could ask: what are the socio-economic implications of lack of POC funding in advancing scientific ideas to the market?

Drawing on research that looks at this issue in high-income countries, some have pointed at the fundamental incompatibility between the instrumental role of POC in advancing scientific ideas to the market and the persistent reluctance of investors to have prototyping funded (Portilla, Evans, Eng, & Fadem, 2010). Wright, Lockett, Clarysse, and Binks (2006) formally consider, using pecking order theory, that there is a mismatch between the demand and supply side of the market as VCs prefer to invest after the seed stage, while TTOs see venture capital as more important than internal funds early on.

The persistent reluctance of investors to have prototyping funded

Although the amounts of POC funding required are small, from the investor perspective, the risks inherent in the very purpose of POC funding greatly reduce the potential for generating direct returns other than reputational ones. Thus, in the longer term, a POC investment could generate opportunities for seed investment in start-ups and, ultimately, equity investment. Another common misleading perception among VCs is that POC is not an area for private sector-led investment activity, and that a POC investor needs nerves of steel because of the very high likelihood of seeing potential returns evaporated. For this very inaccurate reason, private investors tend to show high risk aversion to participate in early-stage funding and consider that holding an equity stake in a start-up is a high-risk investment which often leads to a long-term illiquid asset.

VCs are key stakeholders in the innovation process, and POC funding can only fulfil their investment purpose when a clear vision between the end-goals and the starting point to achieve them becomes real. The risks for any investor are – by definition – very high: if a concept fails to be proved, the investment is written off as a failure, and the money, whether public or private, is regarded as wasted (West, 2001). However, POC investors should consider that the likelihood of seeing potential returns will increase if the POC portfolio is well managed (as it will be shown in the following chapters).

Lack of funding is therefore a limitation to innovation as public intervention frequently mimics private investment approaches looking for "winners", rather than helping to build a cohort of progressing technologies to be tested in crucial POC experiments (Blum, Manning, & Srivastava, 2012). Technology transfer offices in high-income countries are already trying to address the socio-economic implications of lack of POC funding in advancing scientific ideas to the market. For some, finance should be a catalyst of wealth creation, and yet access to venture capital is a major impediment faced by university spin-out companies seeking to access venture capital (Wright et al., 2006). For others, until VCs cannot realise that the timeframe required to obtain POC investment results (ca. 10–15 years to prove the concepts and demonstrate their commercial potential) is different from VCs' standard investment period (equivalent to the lifetime of a venture capital fund, i.e. ten years), there won't be VCs' interest in making investments in POC and subsequently perpetuate their unwillingness to engage in POC investment.

I posit that POC funding benefits should be perceived beyond the immediate direct returns, as its potential is inherent in the very purpose of POC funding, as in the longer term, it plays a central role in generating a compelling investment pipeline for business angels, seed investors and VCs, and with it opportunities for seed investment in start-ups and, ultimately, VC equity investment.

What happens when competitive markets fail to allocate POC resources efficiently

For public funding, POC is considered an area of "market failure" and, depending on the type of market failure, policy-makers should determine the exact scope and type of government intervention. For authors such as Randall (1983) and Zerbe and McCurdy (2000), market failure occurs when competitive markets fail to allocate resources efficiently and public finance has to make provisions for collective goods (such as research and innovation) management. This cogent observation is reinforced by Mazzucato (2015) who argues that the conventional view of a boring, lethargic state versus a dynamic private sector should move towards a state that intervenes in the economy to fix "market failures" or level the playing field.

Because POC plays a crucial role at the boundary of the public and private sectors in revealing innovative ideas and new technologies that have the potential to progress onto a path of development, both sectors have a visionary role to play in order to imagine and shape the future of innovation. Public sector, for example, should motivate the ecosystem (firms, financial institutions, research and education institutions, public sector funds, intermediaries, the public) to interact in this space, and provide a working framework for all actors involved in the process to stimulate the innovation that the private sector would not try to pursue alone.

An in-depth analysis of the symbiotic innovation system is also required in order to define the boundaries and transform the perceived "market failure" into a crucial space where innovation is shaped and a future investment deal-flow is defined. It has been demonstrated that what drives companies to enter a specific sector in the patent race are the projected technological and market opportunities (Dosi, 1997). Here, it can be effectively argued, based on the Oxford experience and the data presented later in the chapter, that an effective POC activity by entrepreneurial universities is the tipping point of such a move, shaping a new field of business and a new line of long-term investments.

Reasons for university participation in a POC fund

POC funding can only fulfil its purpose when applied with a clear vision of end-goals, and the ways and means to achieve them. As previously underlined, early-stage funding to prove concepts and demonstrate their potential is a vital link on the road to a successful innovation transfer to the market sector, and entrepreneurial universities know it well.

Arguments for university participation in a POC fund need to look beyond generating value from tech-transfer per se, as the potential benefits will also include follow-up grants, industry-sponsored research, an enhanced reputation and a broader educational experience through working relationships with start-ups and SMEs.

In order to have a real impact on tech-transfer, a POC fund has to work from the earliest stages of invention to define goals and appropriate pathways to reach those goals. It is important for a POC fund to bring in industrial expertise, for example, with experienced CEOs interested in working with academic research without losing their links with industry. Cambridge Enterprise's "entrepreneurs in residence" and mentoring models and Harvard's recent "executives in residence" scheme are producing good results by helping universities to understand what industry expects, identify promising projects, clarify their proposals accordingly and build up a viable business model (Pauwels, Clarysse, Wright, & Van Hove, 2016). This is why effective POC deployment depends on high-standard skills to support the process and achieve the financial sustainability of a POC fund, that is, attaining proceeds from outstanding POC portfolio management so as to keep funding the increasing number of eligible IPs experiments.

As mentioned in Chapter 1, the POC fund itself and its staff should be similar in scale to an SME for faster and more efficient networking and team building. The professional competences needed for a POC fund are very much in line with the "soft skills" profile required for successful tech-transfer management: knowledge of the environment to identify the appropriate projects, opportunities and teams to engage in productive collaboration – and the right timing for doing so, high-quality intercultural skills to negotiate between academia and the business world and foster the mutual trust which is essential to efficient working relationships, and the ability to manage expectations so that means can be matched to ends. There is a clear consensus (Finegold, 1999) that people of this calibre and versatility are a rare breed, hard to find and even harder to keep, so commitment is essential. Furthermore, project leaders need a clear overall vision of end-goals as well as "hard skills" that equip them with sufficient knowledge and authority to discuss shareholder expectations and manage conflicts of interest.

Key to the aforementioned aspects is the fund's network of contacts in the business world. On the investment side, POC funding will involve working with players handling small volumes, such as business angels using convertible loans, with a view to follow up funding for the later stages, which can include co-investment, ultimately leading to equity investment. The longer-term view underlying POC funding should also look to the different levels of IP, financial and industrial expertise that will be needed as a tech-transfer project grows.

In developing a POC project, both inventors and investors must be made aware that the time factor can constrain their ambitions, and this varies with different fields of innovation. Academic research would always be viewed as too early a stage to attract interest from short-term investors (Wright et al., 2006): in the life sciences and biomedical technologies in particular, it is difficult, if not impossible, to predict investment outcomes in any given year: the general rule is that, from start to finish, always allow more time than is expected or hoped for.

Advanced TTOs are constantly at work to counterbalance investors' reluctance to invest at an early stage. For this, an effort to be considered in designing a POC fund with the right impact at the right time is the funding application process: if it is not to deter academics, the application should not make disproportionate demands on their time. Close working relationships between the fund and universities are also considered key to optimising the application process for both parties. From the wider perspective of university policy-making to foster POC funding, a fundamental question is whether investment at this crucial stage of the tech-transfer process seeks to de-risk a project or to build it.

Engineering a POC-funded ecosystem – lessons learnt from prominent TTOs

The characteristics of a good POC-funded "ecosystem" cover inputs, ideas, processes and outputs, but also the type of pitfalls which may be encountered, how they can be avoided, the roles of private and public funds and the specific goals which the funds are asked to fulfil. These can include returns on investment, job creation, start-up creation and improving reputations at different levels in the tech-transfer process. Another potential goal is to establish "evergreen" funds, where some of the returns are reinvested into the POC fund.

Can POC-funded ecosystem be engineered, and if so, could this be done on the basis of a territory and even a continent-wide area?

It is crucial in this case to determine not only goals, but also what the territory's strong and weak points are for successful tech-transfer. In France, for example, strong points are excellence in academic research discovery and international knowledge transfer. Here, the SATTs (Sociétés d'Accélération du Transfert de Technologies or Technology Transfer Accelerator Offices) – French technology transfer accelerators offices – were recently introduced to boost innovation-driven business and job creation, with circa €25 billion in public funding granted under the French State's "Investing for the Future" programme, out of which €900 million were dedicated to POC funding (National Research Council, 2009). Models vary according to their environment, but all have the aim of investing in IP rights and POC, introducing a new professional TTO sector across a broad national territory. As regards IP rights, these are managed by the SATTs on behalf of the state: in the case of IDF-Innov (one of the SATTs), the royalties are first used to reimburse the POC funds invested, and the remainder is shared between the university (75%) and the POC fund (25% is ploughed back to sustain the creation of an "evergreen" fund). This approach mimics a similar agreement in force between University of Oxford and the UCSF POC fund.

The experience gained by POC funds in TTOs attached to entrepreneurial universities such as the OUI, Cambridge Enterprise (UK) or Harvard (USA) also illustrates some common characteristics of success in different innovation "ecosystems". These include the cluster-type environment, both virtual and physical, in which they can build up project- and team-based approaches, but also have access to the people skills, business incubators and finance offered by a wider "ecosystem". This is exemplified in the case of the UK's "golden triangle", encompassing Oxford, Cambridge and London, or the Boston area in the USA, where virtuous tech-transfer cycles are being driven by collaboration between universities, start-ups and investors, with early-stage funding to oil the wheels (Mueller, Westhead, & Wright, 2012).

This chapter has provided details of standard services that support IP portfolio management in prominent TTOs, and illustrated, based on the Oxford TTO experience, how POC develops as a key mechanism for successful research commercialisation. Main takeaways from this chapter include the following two: first, that although POC is the least likely to attract private finance, it is vital to shape the pipeline for future investment from the private-led sector, and second, that because POC plays a crucial role at the boundary of the public and private sectors, entrepreneurial universities' TTOs are championing the visionary role that both sectors are called to play in order to imagine and shape the future of innovation; yet, these TTOs cannot do it all alone, and this is why a good POC-funded "ecosystem" is needed. The next chapter will provide details of the POC funding mechanism at the OUI and the best practices followed along the process.

3 POC funding by the University of Oxford TTO

This chapter examines in detail the terms in which the POC funding mechanism of the University of Oxford TTO (OUI) was created and outlines the key operational steps that OUI adopts to successfully deploy and monitor its UCSF POC funding, while also highlighting the features that make this POC funding an innovation-friendly and reliable process. It also touches upon commercialisation (licensing and spin-out) and underlines how at OUI, this normally comes after a careful pre-screening to understand whether or not it is too early to engage with the market to increase chances of positive results.

Academic research is often viewed (Maxwell, Jeffrey, & Lévesque, 2011) as being at too early a stage to attract interest from venture investors or from companies that would develop it further, while conventional public grant schemes rarely support the POC research needed to exemplify university technologies (Oakey, 2003). Consequently, some TTOs tend to start the commercialisation phase too early, by promoting the part of the IP portfolio that is not developed adequately. To plug this gap, the University of Oxford TTO (OUI) uses POC as a tool for IP commercialisation.

POC funding deployed by TTOs (for prototyping) accelerates the commercialisation of innovations out of the university and into the marketplace by providing early funding to novel, early-stage research that most often would not be funded by any other conventional source. Figure 3.1 shows the crucial role of POC in the investment process.

Public and private sectors together have a visionary role to play in imagining and shaping the future of innovation funding. Yet, as mentioned earlier in Chapter 2, lack of funding is often a limitation for innovation, as frequently public intervention replicates private investment approaches, looking for "winners" rather than helping to build the cohort of progressing technologies to be tested in crucial POC experiments.

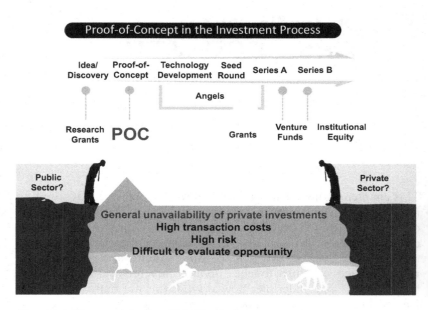

Figure 3.1 The crucial role of POC in the investment process.

On a point of private investment approaches, Mazzucato's view (2015) is that venture capital and early-stage technology investors should not be expected to invest in protecting the intellectual property as it might take five to ten years from the initial filing for a successful POC to shape an investment opportunity for private investors. Figure 3.2 shows the impact of POC in the innovation process.

Some writers, such as Ghosh and Nanda (2010), agree with Mazzucato and highlight the fact that the problem is unlikely to be solved without the active involvement of the government (as discussed in Chapter 2). For example, picking out the winner at an early stage is impossible for VCs, because they tend to focus on the short- to medium-term exit, which is statistically very rare in investment at POC level. Largely, investors are discouraged by the risky nature of POC projects, and tend to fund later-stage companies (Kanniainen & Keuschnigg, 2004).

A point that has also been debated in the literature is whether it is more important to allow VCs to pick the best early-stage technology for further development or to allow a university to develop internal funds to shape the pipeline for progressing investment opportunities

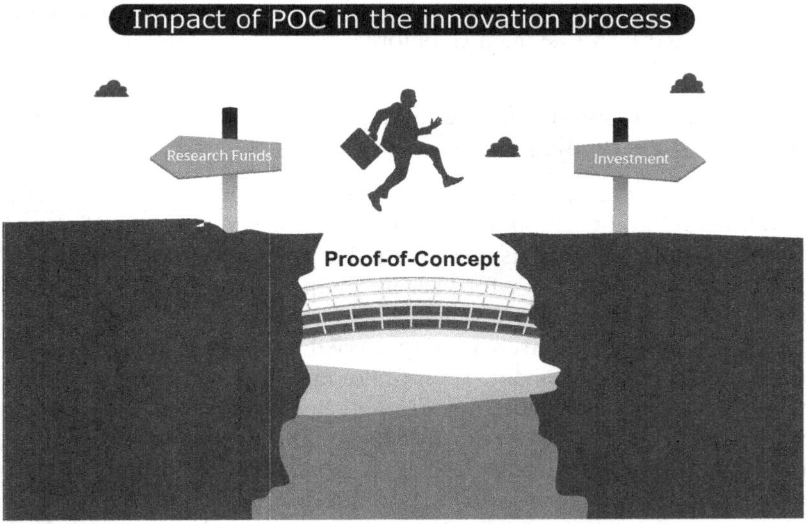

Figure 3.2 Impact of POC in the innovation process.

(Baum & Silverman, 2004). In the green energy sector, for example, while there are several start-ups in clean energy that are well-suited to the traditional venture capital investment model, structural challenges related to VC investment include the inability of VCs to exit their investments at the appropriate time (Ghosh & Nanda, 2010).

A similar problem existed in biotechnology and communications networking when they first emerged, but was ultimately overcome by changes in the innovation ecosystem. However, duties and responsibilities in the oil and power sector are different in two respects. First, they are producing a commodity and hence face little end-user pressure to adopt new technologies. Second, they do not tend to feel as threatened by potential competition from clean energy start-ups, given the market structure and regulatory environment in the energy sector.

This public and private investment approaches dilemma leads to a funding gap, with early-stage companies suffering most. This is why the university's POC funding support at an early stage of the technology development is crucial to progress the embryonic state of a new idea into a marketable product or service for society. The POC funding support offered by the university through its own TTO, therefore, provides the marketable product or service with a negotiating strategic advantage from timely testing, prototyping and exemplification, enabling it to extract value from IP before it becomes obsolete.

How the University of Oxford managed to bridge the early-stage funding gap

By embracing the fact that a POC fund was needed to support the development and exemplification of new ideas (in the form of a patent, copyright, trademarks, design and know-how) into prototypes, in 1999, the University of Oxford set up financial instruments for POC and a logical framework of policies to coordinate the innovation ecosystem around the research activity carried out at the university. This well-managed environment has its foundation on IP protection and follows the rules and procedures established by the university which facilitate the transfer of IP to existing companies or new start-ups willing to develop the technologies into products and services. Through early-funding mechanism, Oxford offers a responsive service to academic research to inspire confidence to the researchers so that their inventions can progress towards the market with the professional help of a dedicated team and a funding scheme, while also increasing the chances of generating financial return from POC activities to further support a growing number of POC project applications.

In order to secure sufficient funding to support POC, the University of Oxford has, in time, created three different POC funds, two of which have now merged under the name of Oxford Invention Fund (OIF) to ask university donors to promote POC across research subjects.

The UCSF was the first POC fund to be set up in 1999, following the UK government initiative to stimulate cooperation between the researchers at universities and the country's industrial entrepreneurs. It was part of the 19 "University Challenge Funds" (UCFs) that were set up to provide funding at the POC stage under the aegis of the government. Interestingly, many UCFs have lapsed, some have been re-established as new seed funds to fund POC projects, while the Oxford fund – the UCSF – is still thriving today.

The UCSF scheme aims to assist university researchers in successfully transforming good research into good business, in bringing university research discoveries to a point where their commercial usefulness can be demonstrated, and the first steps taken to ensure their utility. For the purposes of highlighting what makes the Oxford early-stage funding an innovation-friendly and reliable process, only USCF fund data will be considered.

The UCSF POC portfolio started its formation in the year 2000 as a subset of the IPRs portfolio held by the University of Oxford, which banks more than 5,000 filed patents, copyrights, marks, designs and know-how. This IPRs portfolio, on its own, represents a world-class reservoir of intangible assets that makes Oxford the fifth patent filer in the UK (Sengupta & Ray, 2017).

Such an impressive result stems from a long-standing activity of technology transfer commenced in Oxford in 1988 when the University TTO (OUI, formerly Isis Innovation) inaugurated its activity as an external commercial company wholly owned by the university with the mandate of becoming the TTO of the University of Oxford. Since the launch of UCSF, more than 200 POC projects have been presented and discussed. Here, following, the POC, funding process at OUI is presented in detail.

POC funding application at OUI – an innovation-friendly and reliable process

The POC application process at OUI is defined to foster POC projects with high probability to generate further IP (foreground IP). To this end, the TTO assists researchers/inventors in a timely way to identify the IP and protect it. In general, the best practices adopted by OUI to manage a POC project application process are as follow:

- Disclosure of the POC project outline by the IP inventor(s) to the TTM,
- Setting up of the POC project team (researcher/inventor and TTM) to look after every single detail of the emerging IP and confidentially manage the progress of the POC project until its completion,
- POC project drafting according to the guidelines set out in the application form,
- Signing of the agreement with the university lab (or an external one) to carry out the crucial experiment subject to availability of funding,
- Exploring potential early interest of the industry of reference in order to fine-tune the POC project proposal,
- Defining the POC project budget.

POC funding, as any other mechanism used at OUI to promote innovation, is based on innovation-friendly procedures to support each different stage of the application process. In order to show how the

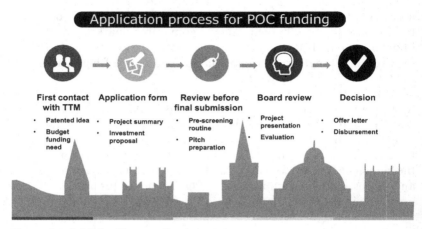

Figure 3.3 POC funding application process.

process is structured, each step of the process will be examined in detail. Figure 3.3 shows the steps of the POC funding application process at OUI.

First contact with a technology transfer manager

The POC application process at OUI begins with drafting of the relevant form by the researcher/inventor as a formal procedure to request POC funding (to UCSF) and establish the first contact with an OUI technology transfer manager, who will then assist (if the POC project has the necessary conditions to be financed). The form is a useful tool to start defining in detail the prototyping project and its budget of an already-patented idea. The application form can be found online on OUI website.

Application form to define POC investment proposal

The draft of the POC application form submission entails that researcher/inventor, together with the guidance of the designated TTM, choose among the POC investment types offered, listed in Figure 3.4, depending on the type of project. Based on this, both the project summary and the POC investment proposal are shaped and handed over to the UCSF manager for review.

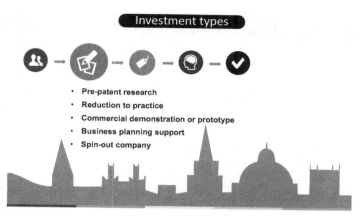

Figure 3.4 POC investment types offered by OUI.

Review before final submission: POC pre-screening routine

The reliable nature and characteristics of POC investments are defined when the POC project proposal generates positive answers to the three guiding questions presented in Figure 3.5.

The POC pre-screening routine allows technology transfer managers to understand whether or not the proposal fulfils the minimum requirements and is eligible to be presented to the POC Investment Advisory Board. Some practical examples for each question are highlighted:

- Does the POC project address a funding gap?

This is a typical situation in which, on the one hand, the research that has generated (IP) has been concluded (status A) and is now ready to be filed; on the other hand, private investors, business angels and VCs believe that the generated IP is still at an embryonic stage and its commercial potential is not clearly visible. If this is the situation, then the answer is YES.

- Is the POC funding able to move the status of the project from A (end of research) to B (initial interest from the market)?

If the structure of the POC project is such that the working prototype or the crucial experiment will lead to practical simplification of the IP,

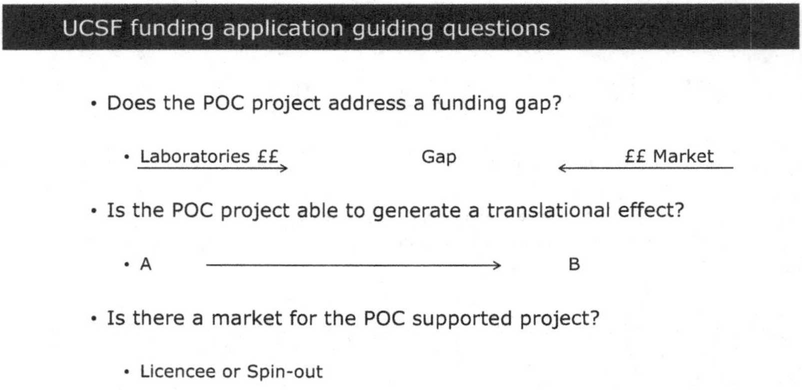

Figure 3.5 POC funding application guiding questions.

for example, into a prototype and possibly to further foreground IP, then the answer to the question is YES.

•   Is there a market for the product or service for which the POC project is aiming to demonstrate the commercial viability?

If it is possible to identify a commercial interest, existing or potential, for the product or service based on the background IP for which one wants to prove the concept, then the answer to the question is YES.

POC project proposal revision before final submission

In order to gain crucial feedback by the University POC Investment Advisory Board, applicants are guided by a TTM to prepare the presentation to pitch the project. The presentation should be no longer than ten slides, as the slot for each project presentation is 30 min (split in 15 min pitching and 15 min Q&A with the board members). The presentation's typical sequence is as follows:

i   brief opening description as an introduction with the project aims,
ii   list of objectives and project plan with clear deliverables from the team and a timeline for the POC project,
iii concise summary of the scientific and technological originality of the proposed POC project,
iv   brief presentation of the research group's work in contrast with other approaches,

v intellectual property (IP) claims and its strength,

vi POC team members' credentials and track records in similar projects,

vii size of the commercial opportunity with risks and rewards of the proposed investment,

viii investment request and expected return to the POC fund.

POC Investment Advisory Board review

The structure of the POC Investment Advisory Board at Oxford consists of the chairman of OUI, the university finance director, an independent non-academic member and four academic members from Scientific University Departments. Members of the committee do not have a fixed-term mandate. The participation of non-academic members is unpaid and perceived as a reputation-enhancing reward. The members of the POC Investment Advisory Board at Oxford and, similarly, at Cambridge bring a wealth of experience and knowledge from both industry and academia.

Following a standard corporate approach, the POC Investment Advisory Board convenes at Oxford quarterly to review POC proposals (on average three, but up to six, per session) and approve or reject investments. This work has been carried out at Oxford without interruption since the year 1999 when the UCSF was created.

The POC Investment Advisory Board meetings at OUI follow an agenda set by the head of the New Venture Support and Funding, who is also in charge of providing the board with a short update on the portfolio management. The POC project proposals (as in the application form) considered eligible for board review after the pre-screening process are distributed to the POC Investment Advisory Board members two weeks before the meeting. The board starts examining the POC investment proposals in sequence (see summary of the Advisory Board Evaluation process in Figure 3.6).

During the meeting, applicants are expected to make a presentation of the POC project to the board as part of the POC funding application. At the end of each project presentation, the chairman of the board invites the applicants to leave the room and asks board members for their decisions.

After a short discussion that follows the presentation, the board normally issues its decision to the applicant on the spot. In either case, whether of approval or rejection, immediate feedback is given to the applicants. In the case of a negative outcome, the OUI staff will detail the feedback to the applicant so that they can redraft the proposal, when pertinent. In the case of a positive outcome, an offer letter is issued.

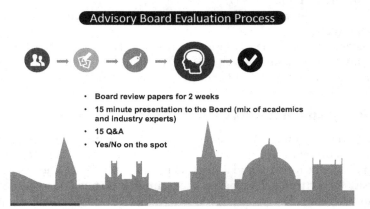

Figure 3.6 Summary of the Advisory Board Evaluation process.

POC Investment Advisory Board decision

The offer letter is the outcome of a successful POC application and embodies the best practices followed at each step of the POC application process and evaluation, which lead to the implementation of the crucial experiment aimed at providing the IP with scalability and competitive advantage (see Figure 3.7).

The successful applicant, researcher at the University of Oxford and inventor of the IP, receives a standard offer letter that sets the terms of the award. The letter is short and written in simple terms. It is nonetheless a contract between the university and the inventor who assumes the obligation, in the case where the work financed by the grant is successful, to convert the award into shares of the future start-up. In order to make this contract financially attractive for the inventor, the conversion price is set *pari passu*, with the share price paid by the future external seed investor in the start-up.

The POC award money will be transferred in full or in tranches from the university account where the UCSF fund monies are held into the university department account where the POC project is going to be developed. Unlike some accelerators, at OUI, there is no central shared laboratory space; each of the funded researchers continues to carry out their study in their own respective laboratory within the university. In the case where the crucial experiment (or prototyping) is performed outside the university laboratory, the funds are transferred to OUI which will manage the contract with the external provider on behalf of the inventor.

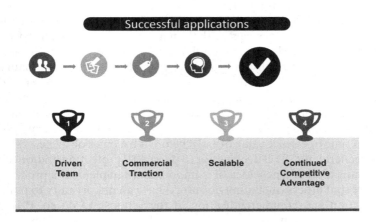

Figure 3.7 Cumulative value of successful POC application.

POC funding monitoring

There are many obstacles when evaluating the performance of POC funds with respect to quantitative metrics of success. Main reasons are as follows: first, because existing iconic POC funds data series are not either published or sufficiently consolidated to evaluate full cycle of a significant sample of POC projects; second, because there are no agreed conventional benchmarks to define POC performance success. While the formation of a business or the licensing of a technology is easy to identify as a success, it is difficult to determine failures. For example, if a researcher receives funding and ultimately discovers that there is no clear market opportunity for a particular technology, this allows the researcher to obtain quicker feedback and begin working on new technologies. However, from the investment point of view, the common wisdom perception would be that the POC money invested has been lost; and, third, because there is no quantitative way to measure how much faster a particular technology reached the market by using a POC award or other intangibles, such as the likelihood that a university innovator (researcher or inventor) will pursue an entrepreneurial endeavour later in life. Moreover, certain technologies require more time than others to develop, and cross-industry comparisons must account for market conditions that are unique to each industry.

Spin-out – commercialisation after POC funding

IP can be commercialised via free distribution, licensing or through new companies (spin-outs or start-ups) that develop and exploit it.

Licensing and spin-out commercialisation at OUI, as advanced earlier in this chapter, normally comes after a careful consideration of whether or not it is too early to engage with the market. In the case of an IP which is not yet developed adequately, OUI would normally first deploy POC as a key IP commercialisation mechanism to plug this gap. Two main results are anticipated with this mechanism: (i) the university increases the chances that a larger percentage of the income stream from the commercialisation of innovations is secured by the TTO, and (ii) a negotiating strategic advantage is built from testing, prototyping and exemplification in time to extract value from IP before it becomes obsolete.

In general, if a TTO decides not to pursue IP protection and/or commercialisation of a new idea, it is important to implement a process to ensure that others (including inventors) have an opportunity to pursue protection and commercialisation, if they choose to do so. Priority must be given to inventors, in this case. However, given the objectives of this research, IP commercialisation via free distribution by the TTO will not be treated here.

Licence agreement between university and industry partners

Once one or more industry partners are identified to market the technology, negotiation of legal contracts (licence agreements) with these industry partners to transfer IP rights of the innovation in exchange for royalties or other considerations becomes crucial. The goal is to negotiate a fair arrangement that facilitates and assists the commercial partner in successfully developing and marketing the product, rather than simply seeking to negotiate the highest fees and royalties in the agreement. Developing industry partnerships can lead to many unexpected benefits for the university, such as sponsored research, student employment opportunities, consulting opportunities and even philanthropic donations to the institution.

Maintaining and managing administrative functions in support of the primary functions of IP protection and technology transfer is of paramount importance to managing the licence agreements. These functions can include accounting, royalty distributions, licensee performance management and patent application management.

Establishing a university spin-out or start-up

Establishing successful new companies (also called spin-outs or start-ups) requires the following: making sure that the project is close enough to the market, there is a coordinated team of professionals with a solid business plan to implement and, finally, proper measuring of the market traction.

Making sure that the project is close enough to the market

Once the POC project has been funded and completed, at the end of the prototyping project, it is fundamentally important to assess if the project has reached status B (initial interest from the market), close enough to the market to generate interest from investors or licensees.

This analysis is vital to understand the power of prototyping and the business story associated with it in order to convince the private-led sector to provide further funding. If not, the POC team might decide that is necessary to design an additional POC step to achieve status B needed to prove the concept. If yes, then that is the right moment to form a spin-out (or start-up) team with possibly an external manager (CEO designate) to develop a business plan and a full business story to be presented as an initial pitch to investors.

Setting up a management team to implement the business plan

Establishing successful new companies (also called spin-outs or start-ups) requires the following: a solid business plan, a coordinated team of professionals who share a common vision, and TTMs who act as mediators in the spin-out process. The help of TTMs at this stage is crucial to bridge the cultural divide that often exists between the spirit of researchers/inventors of IP and that of an entrepreneur for the formation of a new company.

New companies – regardless of whether they are spin-outs from universities or larger companies, or stand-alone start-ups – have little momentum as they are usually understaffed and lack adequate resources. While new start-ups' management teams are still developing, these companies themselves have no established market position, and they have the difficult job of convincing potential investors that they have a positive/lucrative future. This means that single-minded management direction and maximum efficiency are essential for such a company to even survive its first few years, let alone develop a strong position in its field.

Once the POC stage has been completed, another step that is important to address in order to progress the IP to the market is the team formation when the commercialisation takes the spin-out route. There is consensus that the active involvement of the inventor is critical to the success of the licensing and (especially) spin-out process. Faculty researchers need to be actively incentivised to participate in technology transfer; postgraduate students need to be encouraged to stay on at universities and placed in an environment in which their entrepreneurial instincts can flourish. In Oxford, this is helped by the (Said) Business School and other independent incubators.

In most cases, commercial success is more likely to happen if the inventor remains enthusiastically engaged with the project. The inventor, though, does not need to be in charge of the process; indeed, inventors are not usually the best people to implement commercial development plans. However, they should remain active partners of the plan: not only can they prevent the repetition of unsuccessful experiments ("blind alleys"), but their creativity can be used to solve problems that may arise as commercialisation proceeds.

The company employees need not be close friends, but they should respect each other. Choosing a respected managing director is especially important, since the director will implement the business plan. This plan must be clear and succinctly describe how the business will make money. What is the company going to sell? Where is it going to obtain the resources? Who is it going to sell the finished products to, and how? Providing the answers to these questions will require both intelligent leadership and business acumen, which are obvious essential traits of a managing director.

Measuring the market traction

Measuring the market traction of a specific POC project after funding and assessing the value of the POC activity already performed is particularly useful for TTOs to determine their POC portfolio performance. In Chapter 4, this will be touched upon when measuring the OUI POC portfolio exits.

This chapter has described how the University of Oxford early-stage funding was created to successfully deploy and monitor POC, prototyping and crucial exemplification experiments. The case of UCSF, one of the university-dedicated POC funds, was examined to highlight the features that make Oxford early-stage funding an innovation-friendly and reliable process. The POC funding process was unpacked to underline how commercialisation (licensing and spin-out) should follow a careful pre-screening in order to avoid premature engagement with the market and increase commercialisation results. Main takeaways from this chapter include, first, that the UCSF POC portfolio is a subset of the IPRs portfolio held by the University of Oxford, which banks more than 5,000 filed patents, copyrights, marks, designs and know-how, and, on its own, represents a world-class reservoir of intangible assets that makes Oxford the fifth patent filer in the UK; second, that unlike some TTOs that start promoting (often unsuccessfully) the part of the IP portfolio that is not developed adequately, Oxford TTO (OUI) uses POC as an effective mechanism for IP commercialisation. In the next chapter, the results of the POC funding at OUI will be quantified and discussed to emphasise two elements of success: in terms of revenues and in the number of connections between POC projects.

4 POC investment portfolio analysis

This chapter presents the results of the quantitative analysis carried out to measure the success that POC funding has generated in 15 years of IP portfolio management by the University of Oxford TTO (OUI). For the purposes of this work, only one of the POC funds of the University of Oxford, the University Challenge Seed Fund (UCSF), has been considered, as it offered the most complete set of data for the period of analysis. The UCSF POC funding success is here measured taking into account two definitions: (i) success as a function of income and (ii) success as a function of project-project connections. For methodological purposes, the POC projects analysed were collected into groups known as "idea clouds". Information relevant to individual UCSF POC projects has been obtained from a comprehensive review of university sources, including annual activity web posting, quarterly Advisory Board meetings information released on published reports and/or webpages and personal interviews with OUI and POC project teams.

The cumulative financial result that has led the UCSF fund to be "in the money" has also been considered, and it has been calculated by comparing the sum of the proceeds from the sale of portfolio shares with the initial fund size (or the total money given to the fund to begin its operations). The financial results achieved by OUI through IP portfolio management outline the instrumental role that POC funding plays as an effective mechanism to accelerate the IP commercialisation process, while unleashing innovation, generating a multiplier effect in terms of fundraising, providing customisable support to the university researchers and increasing the ability to fill early-stage funding gaps.

The cumulative financial analysis covers a period of 15 years (around the period between 2000 and 2016) of POC funding at OUI, and its results are presented in tables, graphs and figures to illustrate UCSF POC portfolio progression from a status A (end of research) to a status B (initial interest from the market), and then to exit. The analysis brings evidence about TTOs IP management performance and fills a gap in the tech-transfer field where historical data are, in general, scarce. This analysis finding may also be of great value for research institutions and practitioners interested in assessing POC performance.

The outcomes of this comprehensive analysis aim to validate the operative procedures and best practices observed by OUI to test, prototype and exemplify the technology (as set out in Chapter 3) as a way of accelerating IP commercialisation out of the university and into the marketplace. They also wish to demonstrate that relatively small sums invested in POC can produce a substantial translational effect that helps build, over time, a sound POC pipeline to effectively progress new technologies from early adopters to later-stage traditional investors. Measuring the extent to which prototyping experiments increase the ability of the university IP portfolio to reach the market helps a TTO to identify the moment when an IP becomes the initial asset of a new start-up or a commercial licence. This POC funding quantification, therefore, brings unique evidence in the effort to discern why, in general, too many patents fail to turn into licences; too few licences turn into significant earners.

Measuring UCSF funding success as a function of income

In order to quantify the outcomes of OUI portfolio management as a function of income, a fundamental question emerges: how much does UCSF return to the university following funding?

Looking at the operative side, since the beginning of its operations, for 15 years, the UCSF has provided funds of over £8.4 million across 157 projects from 216 applications (OUI publication, 2015). It is a gender unbiased funding mechanism, and it has awarded funding indistinctively towards projects led by both male and female applicants. In addition, the UCSF has sponsored a wide range of projects across the university (see Figure 4.1), thus contributing to driving innovation in several sectors.

For this income perspective of success, OUI POC projects were collected into groups, known as "idea clouds" (Figure 4.2). The advantage of an idea cloud is the ability to collect income and funding from multiple projects. This is especially important in cases where related or "child" projects generate income (Leem, 2015).

For instance, if project "X" was given UCSF funding, it is possible that project "X" did not provide direct return (or there is no record to justify the claim). However, a new project "Y" may have been built upon the IP of project "X", leading to a new spin-out. In this case, it is debatable whether "X" had established the necessary platform for "Y". Therefore, any amount of economic return generated by "Y" is collected into the idea cloud with both "X" and "Y".

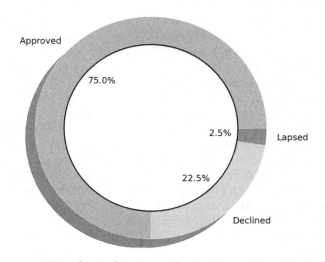

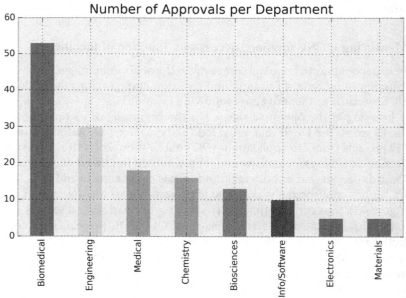

Figure 4.1 Percentage of POC applications approved, declined or lapsed and number of approvals according to department/field.

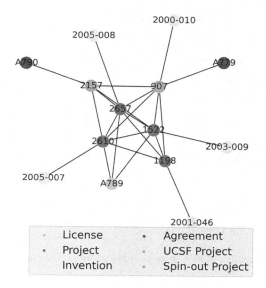

Figure 4.2 Idea cloud of a UCSF project.

Each idea cloud's income is the sum of its constituent projects' income. Thus, if an idea cloud has four projects, the idea cloud's income is the sum of the incomes of its four projects. The majority of UCSF idea clouds did not produce any economic return (see Figure 4.3). Forty-four realised some cash value, and 23 were "profitable". In particular, five idea clouds returned over £1 million.

In order to determine if UCSF funding had influenced the level of income, the income distribution from UCSF idea clouds was compared to the income distribution from non-UCSF idea clouds (which are IP projects that had not benefitted from POC funding at all). The two income distributions were significantly different (Mann–Whitney U test: $p < 0.001$; Figure 4.4). The shapes of the distributions suggest that UCSF-funded idea clouds tend to return more to the university.

Measuring USCF funding success as a function of project-project connections

The question that emerges here is as follows: does a UCSF-funded project lead to subsequent project disclosures?

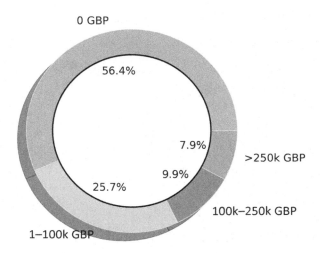

0 GBP

56.4%

7.9%

9.9%

25.7%

>250k GBP

100k–250k GBP

1–100k GBP

Figure 4.3 Percentage of POC idea clouds yielding different bands of income.

For this perspective of success, projects were also collected into the groups known as "idea clouds" (similar to Figure 4.2). The advantage of an idea cloud in this case is that it is especially important in cases where data sources refer to the same spin-out with different project numbers (Leem, 2015).

The idea clouds find another advantage when one spin-out (or idea) has multiple project numbers. And again, an idea cloud is said to be a "UCSF idea cloud" if any projects within the cloud were funded by UCSF; otherwise, the idea cloud is classified as a "non-UCSF" idea cloud.

The success of UCSF was also measured by the number of project nodes in the idea cloud. Similar to that mentioned/shown earlier, the number of project nodes in UCSF and non-UCSF idea clouds were compared to each other using the Mann–Whitney U test[1] (Figure 4.4). The distributions of the number of projects are different ($p < 0.001$); about 25% of UCSF idea clouds have at least three projects. In contrast, only 2% of non-UCSF idea clouds have as many projects (Figure 4.5).

Despite the fact that UCSF idea clouds tend to have more projects, it is difficult to establish a causal relationship. In order to infer a causal relationship (should it exist), more data are necessary – for instance, the number of projects that were disclosed following funding.

Other definitions of success were explored; however, they were not productive. For example, the distribution of time elapsed between the

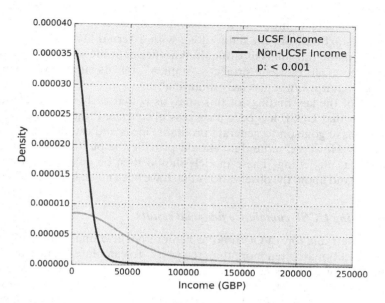

Figure 4.4 Income density curves for UCSF and non-UCSF idea clouds.

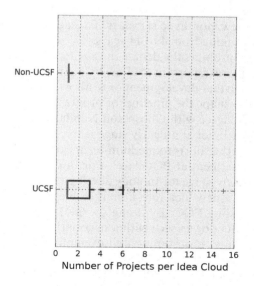

Figure 4.5 Distributions of the number of projects in UCSF and non-UCSF idea clouds.

start of a project until the start of a licence agreement was used to measure the "speed" of innovation. As mentioned, the ubiquitous nature of project start dates in the data, along with external factors (e.g. legal issues), made this analysis difficult. Another definition, which we had hoped to explore, was a project's "impact", but its subjective nature meant that it was not precisely quantifiable.

One of the key findings of this analysis is that early-stage evidence suggests that UCSF has been a successful scheme. Projects funded by UCSF have gone on to generate profitable ideas and establish links to projects. However, more data should provide the platform for future statistical modelling. These models should then be able to reinforce, and expand upon, the observations that have been made in this analysis.

Measuring UCSF cumulative financial results

The timeframe for a POC fund to achieve positive financial results is unconventional, often more than ten years. To calculate the number of years that were necessary to progress 157 UCSF POC projects from A (end of research) to B (initial interest from the market), and then to exit at OUI, data sourced from OUI Report (2016) and relevant projects press releases for exit of UCSF POC-funded projects between 2000 and 2016 were used. The results show that on average, 1.3 years are necessary to reach status B, with a time spent for individual project ranging from a few months to six years. To reach exit, it took, on average, 9.6 years, ranging from 4 to 14 years.

This outcome prompts the debate in the literature (in Chapter 3) as to whether it is more important to allow VCs to pick the best early-stage technology for further development or to allow a university to develop internal funds to shape the pipeline for progressing investment opportunities. I would agree with Ghosh and Nanda's (2010) statement that picking out the winner at an early stage is impossible for VCs as they tend to focus on the short- to medium-term exit, which is statistically very rare in investment at POC level. For this reason, OUI strategically supports early-stage technology development to progress the embryonic state of a new idea into a marketable product or service for society by providing POC. By doing so, OUI provides the resulting marketable product or service with a negotiating strategic advantage from timely testing, prototyping and exemplification, enabling it to extract value from IP before it becomes obsolete.

The following analysis of OUI POC funding data for the period between 2000 and 2016 offers an invaluable opportunity to measure UCSF cumulative financial result by comparing the sum of the proceeds from the sale of portfolio shares with the initial fund size (or the total money invested at the beginning of its operations). This measure is also commonly used for evergreen funds to establish whether or not they have reached financial success.

The results indicate that the £4 million given to the university in 1999 to start POC funding operations has been doubled by the exit incomes, which were ploughed back in total into the fund to award – as at December 2015 – nearly £8.4 million in grants (OUI publication, 2015). This substantiates the fact that after 15 years of POC funding, the UCSF was "in the money".

Besides, UCSF had already seen over 50 spin-out companies raise over £90 million in seed capital (OIU publication, 2015), which means that UCSF has also generated a multiplier effect in terms of fundraising. Moreover, the number of spin-outs has increased rapidly over the 15 years, as a result of evolving POC translational effect and the entrepreneurial culture of the university, accentuated by the entrepreneurial propensity of the academics and scientists in University of Oxford, which is one of the largest generators of spin-outs in the UK.

Assessing the value of UCSF POC funding process in successful IP commercialisation

As anticipated in Chapter 3, a quantitative analysis of OUI POC management will be considered to highlight the value that each step of the UCSF funding process adds to the ability of the university IP portfolio to reach the market successfully. This detailed data analysis also aims to ratify the prominent role that POC funding plays in strengthening procedures and best practices put in place to accelerate the IP commercialisation process, while providing customisable support to researchers and the ability to fill early-stage funding gaps.

Annual UCSF funding trends – from application to award

Table 4.1 summarises, on a financial year basis, the UCSF portfolio investment activity between 1999 and 2015 – from application to disbursement of award. It shows that the annual average investment size (between £25,000 and £250,000) is a proxy for the POC gap to move a project from A (end of research) to B (initial interest from the market). This average investment size not only demonstrates that relatively small sums invested in POC are instrumental in unleashing innovation, but also that they are capable of generating a multiplier effect in terms of fundraising by allowing over 50 university spin-out companies to

Table 4.1 USCF portfolio investment activity (1999–2015)

Year	Application value (£)	Award value (£)	Number of awards	Average award value (£)
1999	–	–	–	–
2000	2,143,073	1,145,655	22	52,075
2001	1,621,474	780,465	22	35,476
2002	1,908,642	1,582,683	20	79,134
2003	471,110	471,110	4	117,778
2004	–	–	–	–
2005	–	–	–	–
2006	491,558	454,558	8	56,820
2007	876,600	426,173	13	32,783
2008	1,045,996	637,788	9	70,865
2009	580,564	412,080	9	45,787
2010	779,018	456,775	11	41,525
2011	419,555	354,255	7	50,608
2012	228,698	190,974	3	63,658
2013	215,000	50,000	1	50,000
2014	1,473,168	1,056,129	14	75,438
2015	1,465,425	854,506	14	61,036

Source: Oxford University Innovation, 2015.

raise over £90 million in seed capital. Furthermore, this confirms that POC funding is vital to trigger a successful tech-transfer process. The results also highlight the fundamental roles of POC funds at OUI in decreasing investment risks and shaping the pipeline for future investments from the private-led sector.

Anecdotal evidence via interviews supports this claim. For example, one project examined was denied funding from a governmental agency, yet received funding from the POC fund of Oxford UCSF. The POC funding allowed the concept to be proved. Once this had occurred, many outside investors became interested in funding the project's further development. Undoubtedly, the success of the POC awards can be seen in the power given grantees to leverage more capital for their technologies. By legitimising a researcher's technology, OUI has enabled and accelerated the acquisition of private capital for university technology.

There are areas where OUI can improve their efficiency and usefulness. For example, some participants in a survey run by OUI criticised the limited POC funding amount allocated and the number of POC proposals funded per year as being too few; however, in general, respondents spoke positively about OUI.

Figure 4.6 shows the annual amount of monies invested by the UCSF (evergreen fund) over 15 years, and the trend it followed between 2000

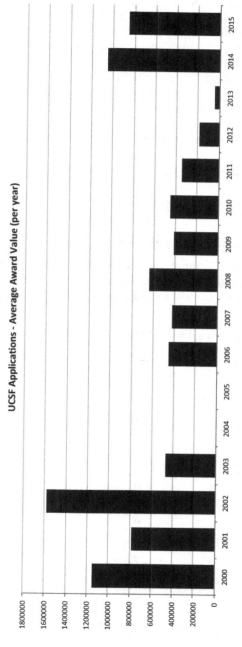

Figure 4.6 The UCSF annual amount of monies invested by the POC fund over 15 years.

and 2015, marking the POC funding phases at OUI. In particular, during the years 2004, 2005 and then in 2012, 2013, the UCSF cash was depleted, which brought about a stop to, or significant reduction of, its investment activity during these critical years. However, given that UCSF is an evergreen fund, the University of Oxford, in 2004, allocated a further £1 million to continue POC operations (under the name of IUIF Fund), using the same investment procedures (same process and offer letter) until some shares in the UCSF portfolio were sold and the proceeds ploughed back into the UCSF money pot, and operations resumed in 2006. This trend makes the Oxford University TTO a typical good POC-funded "ecosystem", as it covers inputs, ideas, processes and outputs, but also pitfalls that may be encountered, how they can be avoided, the roles of private and public funds and what goals the funds are asked to fulfil (see more details in Chapter 2).

Annual UCSF funding – awards versus applications

Table 4.2 shows the annual breakdown of the 157 POC projects awarded out of a total of 216 POC funding applications received between 2000 and 2015. It indicates that the yearly UCSF approval rate

Table 4.2 Annual breakdown of the 157 POC projects awarded

Year	Number of applications	Number of awards	Awarded (%)
1999	–	–	–
2000	32	22	69
2001	32	22	69
2002	27	20	74
2003	4	4	100
2004	0	0	–
2005	0	0	–
2006	10	8	80
2007	16	13	81
2008	17	9	53
2009	12	9	75
2010	15	11	73
2011	8	7	88
2012	3	3	100
2013	1	1	0
2014	18	14	78
2015	21	14	67

Source: Oxford University Innovation, 2015.

of submitted proposals ranges from 65% and above, and that it awards between eight to twelve projects annually. This percentage confirms the soundness of the POC investments pre-screening process at OUI, which is defined by the three guiding questions presented in Chapter 3.

For some experts, TTOs ought not to be profit centres – that is only likely to encourage unrealistic negotiating terms – although they should still be measured on market-driven criteria, such as spin-out profitability and product sales. Such measurement, for the best performers, is likely to encourage universities to focus their energies on the inventions with the greatest potential (Apax Partners, 2005). In my view, the universities should focus their effort in investing in POC to test, prototype and exemplify the technology to produce a substantial translational effect that helps build, over time, a sound POC pipeline to effectively progress new technologies from early adopters to later-stage traditional investors, as UCSF POC fund process has demonstrated.

This chapter has presented the results of the quantitative analysis carried out to measure 15 years of POC funding management by the University of Oxford TTO (OUI). This valuable historical data analysis made it possible to quantify POC funding success. One of the key findings of the analysis suggests that UCSF has been a successful scheme because POC projects funded by UCSF have gone on to (i) generate significant more return to the university when compared to the income distribution from non-UCSF projects (which are IP projects that had not benefitted from POC funding at all), that is, 44 realised some cash value, 23 were "profitable" and five idea clouds returned over £1 million (see Figure 4.3), and (ii) generate profitable ideas and establish project-project connections, that is, comparing the number of project nodes in UCSF and non-UCSF idea clouds, about 25% of UCSF idea clouds have at least three projects. In contrast, only 2% of non-UCSF idea clouds have as many projects.

In relation to the cumulative financial result that has led the UCSF fund to be "in the money", results confirm UCSF funding management success, showing that the £4 million given to the UCSF in 1999 to start operations has been doubled over 15 years by the exit proceeds. More detailed quantitative analysis of OUI POC management also shows that (i) the annual average POC investment size (between £25,000 and £250,000) is relatively small, but instrumental in unleashing innovation and in generating a multiplier effect in terms of fundraising by allowing over 50 university spin-out companies to raise over £90 million in seed capital, and (ii) yearly UCSF approval rate of submitted proposals (ranges from 65% and above) confirms the soundness of the POC investments pre-screening process.

The outcomes of this comprehensive assessment of the UCSF POC funding process sanction that OUI IP portfolio management relies on a well-defined organisational structure to provide capital, guidance and business contacts to university innovators. It also ratifies the instrumental role that UCSF POC funding plays as an effective mechanism to accelerate the IP commercialisation process, while unleashing innovation, generating a multiplier effect in terms of fundraising, providing customisable support to the university researchers and increasing the ability to fill early-stage funding gaps.

Note

1 As defined by Mann and Whitney (1947), the Mann–Whitney U test (also called the Mann–Whitney–Wilcoxon (MWW), Wilcoxon rank-sum test or Wilcoxon–Mann–Whitney test) is a non-parametric test of the null hypothesis that it is equally likely that a randomly selected value from one sample will be less than or greater than a randomly selected value from a second sample. It was considered here because, unlike the t-test, it does not require the assumption of normal distributions. It is nearly as efficient as the t-test on normal distributions to determine whether two independent samples were selected from populations having the same distribution. A similar non-parametric test used on dependent samples is the Wilcoxon signed-rank test.

Conclusions

This book has focused on innovation finance and POC funding in technology transfer. The primary aim was to show that a well-structured TTO can achieve positive financial results from POC funding in the medium-long term, and that the chances for an IP portfolio management to be "in the money" increases if the TTO is attached to an entrepreneurial university. This assumption is confirmed after an extensive literature discussion that brings to the fore the fundamental incompatibility between the instrumental role of POC in advancing scientific ideas to the market and the persistent reluctance of private investors to fund prototypes, worsened by the fact that public intervention frequently replicates private investment approaches.

In the light of the aforementioned, it is not surprising that the university mission is called to fill this gap by generating income from patenting and licensing to self-finance (other than university research and education) university research ideas protection, development and commercialisation as a way to promote economic growth through innovation. In order to exemplify this evolving university role, this book thoroughly examines the emblematic case of the UCSF, which is the POC fund of Oxford. Taking into account the 15-year data available from the University of Oxford, the book estimates the UCSF funding success as a function of both income and project-project connections. Showing, through evidence, that in terms of income, the UCSF tends to return to the University more than the amount initially invested and that in terms of project-project connections, UCSF has generated more profitable ideas than non-UCSF-funded project (IP projects with no POC at all) and established links to projects.

The successful case of UCSF has also allowed to sanction that a TTO-effective IP portfolio management, such as the one championed by OUI, relies on a well-defined organisational structure, innovation-friendly procedures and best practices to provide capital, guidance and business contacts to university innovators. It also ratifies the instrumental role that POC funding plays as an effective mechanism to accelerate the IP commercialisation process, while unleashing innovation, generating a multiplier effect in terms of fundraising, providing customisable support to the university researchers and increasing the ability to fill early-stage funding gaps.

Throughout the four chapters, this book supported this conception, illustrating in details:

i   the salient aspects of the technology transfer evolution from university to society, with particular emphasis on the function that advanced TTOs and highly qualified TTMs play in closing the gap between academia and business, referring to the Bayh Dole Act (enacted in the USA in 1980) as the historical event that propelled this evolution;

ii   how key stages (the dots) of the technology transfer process connect to promote innovation, while generating income from patenting and licensing to self-finance university research, education and to promote economic growth and, based on the Oxford experience, how POC develops as a key mechanism for successful research commercialisation playing a central role in generating a compelling investment pipeline for business angels, seed investors and VCs;

iii the terms in which the Oxford POC fund (UCSF) was created to effectively manage the University IP portfolio (which banks more than 5,000 filed patents and, on its own, represents a world-class reservoir), highlighting the features that make UCSF funding an innovation-friendly and reliable process based on careful pre-screening to understand whether or not it is too early to engage with the market to increase chances of positive and timely licensing and spin-out; and

iv   through facts and figures, the quantification of 15 years of UCSF funding at Oxford taking into account (i) success as a function of income and (ii) success as a function of project-project connections. Sanctioning that early-stage funding is for the University, the most effective mechanism is to accelerate IP commercialisation process, while increasing the ability to fill early-stage funding gaps.

This research has found that a salient aspect of the technology transfer evolution is, from the historical context of innovation theory and practice, the clear linkages between public investment in R&D and the commercialisation of technology. Another aspect underpinning the main transformation of tech-transfer from universities to society is tightly linked to the evolution of licensing in the USA with the enactment of the Bayh Dole Act in 1980. This historical event encouraged universities, within and far afield USA, not to consider IP licensing as an activity which diverted faculty attention from teaching and research but rather as a useful means to secure funding for research beyond public support. From broad literature review, it clearly emerges that IP valorisation has a protagonist position within the process of technology transfer, while TTOs hold the formal mechanism of transferring innovation from research to the private sector for commercial application and public benefit. Advanced TTOs' main features include innovation-friendly procedures and appropriate funding mechanisms to support each different stage of the process. Similarly, a successful technology transfer process requires strong research to generate a sound IP portfolio, a dedicated TTO as a meeting point of science and business and a team of highly skilled TTMs who understand the languages of science and business. If such a process is surrounded by an entrepreneurial ecosystem capable of absorbing innovation and providing ancillary services, then technology transfer is equipped with all its fundamentals to unleash innovation and propel economic growth.

There are downsides, though, in this complex process. The main challenge in the overall process of IP valorisation is that the great majority of ideas, whether protected or not, never make it to the marketplace. In this book, the missing links of the process (of translating innovations into viable products and services) were identified and essentially relate to gaps in the areas of the human factor (skills) and impact funding (for the early stages of POC, prototyping and demonstration).

On a point of skills, it was highlighted in Chapter 1 that technology transfer is all about people, from the inventor of an idea through to the end-customer, once the idea has reached the market. The very rapidly evolving and very diverse landscape of innovation and tech-transfer suggests that formal training required for this category of professionals should include a strong apprenticeship component. This leads also to the issue of scarcity of TTM professionals and the need to consider the kind of reward needed to motivate and/or retain them. Several were considered in this book; nevertheless, probably the most powerful motivator for many TTMs is not financial, but intellectual.

Moving on to understand how impact funding plays a central role in generating a compelling investment pipeline for business angels, seed investors and VCs, findings indicate that lack of financing continues to represent an obstacle, as offering POC to inventors is often a difficult task for most TTOs. In an attempt to explain this, it was found that the fundamental incompatibility between the instrumental role of POC in advancing scientific ideas to the market and the persistent reluctance of investors to have prototyping funded is due to VCs' short investment time horizon, which differs from the long-term investment commitment of university TTOs. Based on this, TTOs mission is to fill the gap while generating income from patenting and licensing to self-finance university research, education and to promote economic growth. Leveraging on the case of a successful TTOs, such as OUI, this book shows how crucial was for Oxford to deploy POC funding as a key mechanism not to start IP commercialisation too early, a factor which normally reduces the chances of achieving full positive financial results.

In the search of evidence to demonstrate through facts and figures how in 15 years of POC investment a successful TTO (OUI) has achieved such a cumulative financial result that has led to the UCSF fund being "in the money" where others have failed, this book presented the results of the quantitative analysis carried out to measure 15 years of IP portfolio management by the University of Oxford TTO (OUI). This valuable historical data analysis made it possible to quantify POC funding success: as a function of income and as a function of project-project connections. One of the key conclusions of this analysis suggests that the UCSF has been a successful scheme because POC projects funded have gone on to generate (i) as a function of income, significant more return to the university when compared to the income distribution from non-UCSF projects (which are IP projects that had not benefitted from POC funding at all) and (ii) as a function of project-project connections, more profitable ideas and established project-project connections; that is, comparing the number of project nodes in UCSF and non-UCSF idea clouds, about 25% of UCSF idea clouds have at least three projects. In contrast, only 2% of non-UCSF idea clouds have as many projects. Moreover, 44 realised some cash value, 23 were "profitable" and five idea clouds returned over £1 million.

Findings also confirm UCSF funding management success by considering the cumulative financial result that has led the UCSF fund to be "in the money". Results show that the £4 million given to the UCSF in 1999 to start operations has been doubled over 15 years by the exit proceeds. This also ratifies that although the annual average POC investment size (between £25,000 and £250,000) was relatively small, it turned instrumental not only in unleashing innovation from embryonic research, but also in generating a multiplier effect in terms of fundraising by allowing over 50 university spin-out companies to raise over £90 million in seed capital.

The outcomes of this comprehensive assessment of the UCSF POC funding process, indeed, sanction that OUI IP portfolio management relies on a well-defined organisational structure to provide capital, guidance and business contacts to university innovators. It also ratifies the instrumental role that UCSF POC funding plays as an effective mechanism to accelerate the IP commercialisation and as a reliable process based on careful POC proposals pre-screening.

Although this data analysis is a valuable benchmark for POC funding, it is worth mentioning that further work should be carried out to compare a larger data set for the benefit of a reinforced statistical modelling. These models might then be able to strengthen, and expand upon, the observations that were made in this book. As a point of clarification, the quantitative analysis offered in this book does not focus on common TTO performance, given the fact that a good TTO performance does not necessarily secure positive financial results solely derived from numbers of patents, licences or spin-outs (O'Shea, Allen, Morse, O'Gorman, & Roche, 2007; Siegel, Veugelers, & Wright, 2007). It is known that these metrics can encourage overly aggressive patenting and do not accurately reflect the long-term commercial impact of transfer activities. For that reason, in this book, the success of UCSF was measured by the number of project nodes in the idea cloud, and the numbers of project nodes in UCSF and non-UCSF idea clouds were compared using the Mann–Whitney U test (1947). It would be beneficial to continue this research by comparing the results obtained for OUI (the TTO of the University of Oxford) with those from other TTOs that hold similar records. This would further validate these conclusions.

Recommendations

TTOs cannot attain everything on their own, even if some try to do so. The expertise of VCs, business angels, alumni, industrialists and other professionals should be systematically leveraged to identify and nurture the technologies with the highest commercial potential. This research has found that although a handful of world class universities, among which is Oxford, are building up relevant innovation-friendly procedures and following best practices to rely on the overall quality of their disclosures to justify a swift approach to patenting and licensing, for most universities, a well-thought-out support is yet needed. This TTO support is crucial not only to close the gap between academia and industry, but also to attract the under-used and under-recognised potential of inventors (males and females) to boost innovation and tech-transfer.

This book established that to reach excellency, highly specialised expertise is required (the human factor played by TTMs) by TTOs and entrepreneurial universities to create and access fluid networks of committed people whose talents, knowledge, money and ideas can be pooled and leveraged. In order to get ready for this, the following are some recommendations:

- develop appropriate training and a recognised qualification for the TTMs professional category, so that it emerges as a network that can champion the appearance of tech-transfer management as a high-value profession,
- ensure that the TTMs qualification has a strong focus on interaction between different cultures (academic/business) and learning through experience,
- start with a teaching-friendly format (classroom learning, e-learning tutorials and locally and/or regionally based training) that can be expanded and reinforced with internships and

mentoring to help build sustained working relationships as well as career prospects, and

- promote the technology transfer management career as part of business school curricula, for example, in order to build up consensus around the idea of launching a certification scheme to build trust in the TTM role among all the players concerned.

In relation to the need of increasing early-stage funding to help sound scientific ideas to cross the chasm (so-called "Valley of Death"), as an obvious way to nurture technologies to the point where venture capital firms and other investors can conduct substantive due diligence on IP commercial prospects (one of the key findings of this work), here are some practical recommendations:

- Innovation finance should be made available, as it can play an important role in the TT process by providing immediate support to new ideas which are only defined embryonically in scientific papers or early IP filings.
- Embryonic scientific ideas often need further development before they can be fully protected as IP in any form (patents, copyright, etc.). This early process normally has necessary costs, and although the amounts are not large, the risks are very high but through a well-managed TTOs these can be minimised.
- To help increase early funding, TTOs and any other innovation agency (dealing with IP, for example) could provide crucial support via Impact Acceleration Funds to start building the bridge over the "Valley of Death", so that for inventors engaging in the technology transfer process the journey moves safely.
- Innovation finance also needs to be made available to continue to move safely from protected ideas to prototypes via POC. This would help further build the bridge and the necessary pipeline to transfer new technologies to start-ups, thus helping shape the future of innovations and the overall purpose of new technologies coming onto the market.
- Putting in place a POC mechanism that secures a reliable pipeline to early-stage investors is of paramount importance to attract them in a growing innovation-led ecosystem. POC is a powerful instrument that provides transparent, secure and non-competitive funding to develop the prototypes, practical demonstrations and crucial experiments required to translate patents or IP elements into marketable products and thus in closing the gap between university research and industry.

- The POC mechanism should always be managed independently (bearing in mind its financial sustainability, e.g. operated as a revolving fund) in order to invest money in inventors' ideas while ensuring that they receive a share of the proceeds if the future business venture is successful.

Last but not least, concerning the need to enlarge and strengthen the underpinning tech-transfer scientific ecosystem and support the bridge over the Valley of Death, my recommendations would be to:

- attract the under-used and under-recognised potential of women to boost innovation and tech-transfer, where at the moment only 15% of patents are filed by women, and
- create an observatory at the transnational political level to track and spot TTM talent, with a particular focus on gender imbalance, which will further contribute the most needed diversity for excellence that technology transfer requires to prosper.

References

Apax Partners Ltd. (2005). *Understanding technology transfer.* London, UK: Apax Partners Ltd/The Economist Intelligence Unit. Retrieved from https://www.wipo.int/export/sites/www/sme/en/newsletter/2011/attachments/apax_tech_transfer.pdf

Baum, J. A., & Silverman, B. S. (2004). Picking winners or building them? Alliance, intellectual, and human capital as selection criteria in venture financing and performance of biotechnology start-ups. *Journal of Business Venturing, 19*(3), 411–436.

Blum, J., Manning, N., & Srivastava, V. (2012). *Public sector management reform: Toward a problem-solving approach.* Washington, DC: Poverty Reduction and Economic Management (PREM) Network Vice-Presidency of the World Bank.

Borrell-Damian, L., Brown, T., Dearing, A., Font, J., Hagen, S., Metcalfe, J., & Smith, J. (2010). Collaborative doctoral education: University-industry partnerships for enhancing knowledge exchange. *Higher Education Policy, 23*(4), 493–514.

Bozeman, B. (2000). Technology transfer and public policy: A review of research and theory. *Research Policy, 29*(4–5), 627–655.

Brint, S. (2005). Creating the future:'New directions' in American research universities. *Minerva, 43*(1), 23–50.

Buxton, B. (2010). *Sketching user experiences: Getting the design right and the right design.* Burlington, MA: Morgan Kaufmann.

Campinos, A. (2018). Speech at the 1st EUIPO Tech-transfer Workshop (author own notes). Alicante, Spain.

Carayannis, E. G., Cherepovitsyn, A. Y., & Ilinova, A. A. (2016). Technology commercialization in entrepreneurial universities: The US and Russian experience. *The Journal of Technology Transfer, 41*(5), 1135–1147.

Cook, T. (2007). The role of technology transfer intermediaries in commercializing intellectual property through spinouts and start-ups. *Intellectual Property Management in Health and Agricultural Innovation: A Handbook of Best Practices.* New York, USA. (Vol. 2, pp. 1289–1294).

Cooper, D. (2014). *Coast to Capital: Strategic Economic Plan Developing Networks of Innovation Space to be Creative* (Report for Coast to Capital Local Enterprise Partnership, Version 1). University of Chichester, West Sussex, UK.

Dosi, G. (1997). Opportunities, incentives and the collective patterns of technological change. *The Economic Journal, 107*(444), 1530–1547.

Etzkowitz, H., Webster, A., Gebhardt, C., & Terra, B. R. C. (2000). The future of the university and the university of the future: Evolution of ivory tower to entrepreneurial paradigm. *Research Policy, 29*(2), 313–330.

Finegold, D. (1999). Creating self-sustaining, high-skill ecosystems. *Oxford Review of Economic Policy, 15*(1), 60–81.

Geuna, A., & Nesta, L. J. (2006). University patenting and its effects on academic research: The emerging European evidence. *Research Policy, 35*(6), 790–807.

Ghosh, S., & Nanda, R. (2010). Venture capital investment in the clean energy sector. *Harvard Business School Entrepreneurial Management Working Paper* (11–020).

Gulbranson, C. A., & Audretsch, D. B. (2008). Proof of concept centers: Accelerating the commercialization of university innovation. *The Journal of Technology Transfer, 33*(3), 249–258.

Handler, R., & Maizlish, B. (2005). *IT portfolio management step-by-step: Unlocking the business value of technology.* Hoboken, NJ: John Wiley & Sons.

Harhoff, D., & Hoisl, K. (2007). Institutionalized incentives for ingenuity—patent value and the German Employees' Inventions Act. *Research Policy, 36*(8), 1143–1162.

Hazelkorn, E. (2009). Community engagement as social innovation. In L. Weber & J. Duderstadt (Eds.), *e Role of the Research University in an Innovation-Driven Global Society.* Economica.

Intellectual Property Institute of Canada (IPIC). (2017). *Facilitating Technology Transfer. Submission to the Standing Committee on Industry, Science and Technology For its Study on Intellectual Property and Technology Transfer.* Ottawa: Intellectual Property Institute of Canada.

Isis Innovation Report. (2010). *Oxford University challenge seed fund 10 year report 1999–2009.* Tech-transfer definition by Cooksey (p. 1). Oxford, UK: Oxford University.

Isis Innovation Report. (2015). *Proof of concept & seed investment funding 15 years of successful support.* Oxford, UK: Oxford University.

Kanniainen, V., & Keuschnigg, C. (2004). Start-up investment with scarce venture capital support. *Journal of Banking & Finance, 28*(8), 1935–1959.

Keay, A. (2007). Tackling the issue of the corporate objective: An analysis of the United Kingdom's enlightened shareholder value approach. *Sydney Law Review, 29*, 577.

Knapp, J., Zeratsky, J., & Kowitz, B. (2016). *Sprint: How to solve big problems and test new ideas in just five days.* New York, NY: Simon and Schuster.

Leem, J. (2015). *UCSF – A successful funding mechanism?* (Internship final report). Oxford, UK: Oxford University.

Mann, H. B., & Whitney, D. R. (1947). On a test of whether one of two random variables is stochastically larger than the other. *The Annals of Mathematical Statistics, 18*(1), 50–60.

Maskus, K. E. (2000). *Intellectual property rights in the global economy.* Washington, DC: Peterson Institute.

Maxwell, A. L., Jeffrey, S. A., & Lévesque, M. (2011). Business angel early stage decision making. *Journal of Business Venturing, 26*(2), 212–225.

Mazzucato, M. (2015). *The entrepreneurial state: Debunking public vs. private sector myths* (Vol. 1). London, UK: Anthem Press.

Merton, R. K. (1968). The Matthew effect in science. *Science, 159*(3810), 56–63.

Mueller, C., Westhead, P., & Wright, M. (2012). Formal venture capital acquisition: Can entrepreneurs compensate for the spatial proximity benefits of South East England and 'star' golden-triangle universities? *Environment and Planning A, 44*(2), 281–296.

National Research Council. (2009a). *An assessment of the SBIR program at the department of defense.* Washington, DC: National Academies Press.

National Research Council. (2009b). *Understanding research, science and technology parks: Global best practices: Report of a symposium.* Washington, DC: National Academies Press.

Oakey, R. P. (2003). Funding innovation and growth in UK new technology-based firms: Some observations on contributions from the public and private sectors. *Venture Capital: An International Journal of Entrepreneurial Finance, 5*(2), 161–179.

O'Shea, R. P., Allen, T. J., Morse, K. P., O'Gorman, C., & Roche, F. (2007). Delineating the anatomy of an entrepreneurial university: The Massachusetts Institute of Technology experience. *R&D Management, 37*(1), 1–16.

Pauwels, C., Clarysse, B., Wright, M., & Van Hove, J. (2016). Understanding a new generation incubation model: The accelerator. *Technovation, 50*, 13–24.

Penrose, E. T., & Zamora, C. (1974). *La economía del sistema internacional de patentes. Economía y Demografía.* México:. Siglo Veintiuno,. 1974. viii, 253 p.; 21 cm. Edición; 1a ed. Universidad Autónoma de Nayarit (UAN), México Biblioteca Central.

Portilla, L. M., Evans, G., Eng, B., & Fadem, T. J. (2010). Advancing translational research collaborations. *Science Translational Medicine, 2*(63), 63cm30. doi:10.1126/scitranslmed.3001636.

Randall, A. (1983). The problem of market failure. *Natural Resources Journal, 23*(1), 131–148.

Robbio, A. (2017). *Tech start-ups: How do you know if your idea is worth pursuing?* [Online article] Forbes Technology Council. Retrieved from https://www.forbes.com/sites/forbestechcouncil/2017/09/29/tech-startups-how-do-you-know-if-your-idea-is-worth-pursuing/#7a36463a1955

Roessner, D., Bond, J., Okubo, S., & Planting, M. (2013). The economic impact of licensed commercialized inventions originating in university research. *Research Policy, 42*(1), 23–34.

Roessner, J. D., (2000). Technology transfer. In C. Hill (Ed.), *Science and technology policy in the US: A time of change.* London: Longman.

Rothaermel, F. T., & Thursby, M. (2005). Incubator firm failure or graduation? The role of university linkages. *Research Policy, 34*(7), 1076–1090.

Rousseau, D. M., Sitkin, S. B., Burt, R. S., & Camerer, C. (1998). Not so different after all: A cross-discipline view of trust. *Academy of Management Review, 23*(3), 393–404. doi:10.5465/amr.1998.926617s.

Roy, R., & Group, D. I. (1993). Case studies of creativity in innovative product development. *Design Studies, 14*(4), 423–443.

Sapsalis, E., de la Potterie, B. V. P., & Navon, R. (2006). Academic versus industry patenting: An in-depth analysis of what determines patent value. *Research Policy, 35*(10), 1631–1645.

Sengupta, A., & Ray, A. S. (2017). Choice of structure, business model and portfolio: Organizational models of knowledge transfer offices in British Universities. *British Journal of Management, 28*(4), 687–710.

Siegel, D. S., & Phan, P. H. (2005). Analyzing the effectiveness of university technology transfer: Implications for entrepreneurship education. In *University entrepreneurship and technology transfer* (pp. 1–38). Bingley, UK: Emerald Group Publishing Limited.

Siegel, D. S., Waldman, D. A., Atwater, L. E., & Link, A. N. (2003). Commercial knowledge transfers from universities to firms: Improving the effectiveness of university–industry collaboration. *The Journal of High Technology Management Research, 14*(1), 111–133.

Siegel, D. S., Veugelers, R., & Wright, M. (2007). Technology transfer offices and commercialization of university intellectual property: Performance and policy implications. *Oxford Review of Economic Policy, 23*(4), 640–660.

Swamidass, P. M., & Vulasa, V. (2009). Why university inventions rarely produce income? Bottlenecks in university technology transfer. *The Journal of Technology Transfer, 34*(4), 343–363.

United States. Office of Scientific Research and Development, & Bush, V. (1960). *Science: The Endless Frontier: A Report to the President on a Program for Postwar Scientific Research: July 1945.* Alexandria, VA: National Science Foundation.

Upton, S. (2010). *Four key uses of prototyping.* MoldMaking Technology [Online Article]. Retrieved from https://www.moldmakingtechnology.com/articles/why-is-prototyping-important

Van Norman, G. A., & Eisenkot, R. (2017). Technology transfer: From the research bench to commercialization: Part 1: Intellectual property rights—basics of patents and copyrights. *JACC: Basic to Translational Science, 2*(1), 85–97.

Walshok, M. L., & Shapiro, J. D. (2014). Beyond tech transfer: A more comprehensive approach to measuring the entrepreneurial university. In *Academic Entrepreneurship: Creating an entrepreneurial ecosystem* (pp. 1–36). Bingley, UK: Emerald Group Publishing Limited.

West, J. (2001). The mystery of innovation: Aligning the triangle of technology, institutions and organisation. *Australian Journal of Management, 26*(1_suppl), 21–43.

Wheaton, B. (2006). Managing a medium-sized technology transfer office. *AUTM Technology Transfer Practice Manual, 2*(1), 9–11.

Wiesner, J. B. (1979). Vannevar Bush. *Biographical Memoirs, 50*, 89.

Wright, M., Lockett, A., Clarysse, B., & Binks, M. (2006). University spin-out companies and venture capital. *Research Policy, 35*(4), 481–501.

Young, T. A., Krattiger, A., Mahoney, R. T., Nelsen, L., Thomson, J. A., Bennett, A. B., … Kowalski, S. P. (2007). Establishing a technology transfer office. *Intellectual property management in health and agricultural innovation: a handbook of best practices, 1/2*, 545–558.

Zerbe Jr, R. O., & McCurdy, H. (2000). The end of market failure. *Regulation, 23*(2), 10.

Index

Note: page numbers followed by "n" denote endnotes.

academia: and innovation 13; and research commercialisation 14; and TTO's mission 14

Advanced Technology Program (ATP) 10

annual UCSF funding: from application to award 57–60; awards *vs.* applications 60–2; trends 57–60

application form, defining POC investment proposal 40–1

apprenticeship-based learning 19

Association of University Technology Managers (AUTM) 10, 18

Bayh Dole Act 9–11, 21, 65

biotechnology 37

Bush, Vannevar 8

business school training 19

Cambridge Enterprise (UK) 33

commercialisation: after POC funding 45–6; of innovations 35; licensing and spin-out 45–6; research 34

communications networking 37

Cooperative Research Development Agreements (CRADAs) 10–11

economic development, and TTO 14–15

Employees' Inventions Act (Germany) 9

engineering, POC-funded ecosystem 33–4

"evergreen" funds 33

Fed Lab T/T Act 10

France: "Investing for the Future" programme 33; technology transfer accelerators offices 33

"hard skills" 3, 32

Harvard (USA) 3, 31, 33

Higher Education Innovation Fund (HEIF) 11

idea protection 24

IDF-Innov (SATT) 33

innovation: and academic excellence 13; and people 16; and technology transfer 12; and tech-transfer process 12; and TTOs 23–5

intellectual property (IP) 1; commercialisation 24; registering 22

invention assessment 24

invention disclosure 23–4

inventors, challenge for securing POC 2–6

"Investing for the Future" programme 33

Isis Innovation 25

licence agreement 25; IP protection and 46; technology transfer 46; between university and industry partners 46

licensing 24; commercialisation after 25; revenue distribution 25

Mann–Whitney *U* test 54, 62n1, 67
Mann–Whitney–Wilcoxon (MWW)
test 62n1

Oxford Invention Fund (OIF) 38

patent protection 24
"people skills" 17
POC-funded ecosystem 33–4
POC funding: commercialisation
after 45–6; monitoring of 45
POC Investment Advisory Board
decision 44–6
POC investment portfolio analysis:
annual UCSF funding 60–2;
annual UCSF funding trends
(from application to award) 57–60;
awards *vs.* applications 60–2;
measuring UCSF funding success
as function of income 51–3;
measuring USCF funding success
as function of project-project
connections 53–7; overview 50–1
POC investment proposal 40–1
POC pre-screening routine 41–2
POC project proposal revision before
final submission 42–3
proof-of-concept (POC) 1; challenge
for inventors to secure 2–6; funding
24, 27–9; as IP commercialisation
mechanism 27–32; resources
allocation 30–1; and technology
transfer 1; and TTO 2; university
participation in funding 31–2; and
venture capitalists 3
prototype: and funding 29–30;
importance of 1; working 1
public investment: and POC 30; in
research & development (R&D) 8
Public Law 96–517 *see* Bayh Dole
Act
publicly funded universities *vs.*
scientific inventions management 9

research commercialisation 34;
commercial approaches to 14;
objectives for 14–15; and university
mission 13–15
research & development (R&D):
public investment in 8

SATTs (Sociétés d'Accélération du
Transfert de Technologies) 33
scientific inventions management *vs.*
publicly funded universities 9
Scottish Executive Expertise,
Knowledge, and Innovation
Transfer Programme (SEEKIT) 11
Second World War (WWII) 9
small and medium-sized enterprises
(SMEs) 16
Society of University Patent
Administrators (SUPA) 10, 18
"soft skills" 2–3
start-up formation 24
STTR programmes 10, 28
support services 23–5

Technology Licensing Office (TLO) 9
technology transfer: challenges of 8;
defined 7; evolution 9–12; faculty
researchers 48; and innovation 12;
licence agreement 46; as people's
business 15–16; and POC 1; role of
7; and "soft skills" 2–3; successful 8
technology transfer managers
(TTMs) 8, 15, 16–21; first contact
with 40; motivating 19–21; POC
pre-screening routine and 41;
qualifications 17; rewarding 19–21;
role of 17–18; training for 18–19
Technology Transfer Offices
(TTOs) 2; and academics 14; and
economic development 14–15;
entrepreneurial universities 34; and
government funding 11; and long-
term investment 3; mission of 66;
POC funding deployed by 35; as
profit centres 61; prominent 33–4;
for prototyping 35; requirements to
consolidate research and industry
networks 12–15; and research
activity 13; and revenue earnings
15; and supporting innovation 23–5

UCSF POC funding 33; process,
assessing value in successful IP
commercialisation 57
universities: on long-term investment
to TTO 15; participation in POC
fund 31–2; publicly funded *vs.*

scientific inventions management 9; and research commercialisation 13–15

University Challenge Seed Fund (UCSF) 38, 50; cumulative financial results 56–7

university companies (UNICOs) 11

University Licensing Professionals 10, 18

University of Oxford: early-stage funding 48–9; IPRs portfolio held by 39; managing to bridge the early-stage funding gap 38–9

University of Oxford TTO (OUI) 3–5, 35–49; application form to define POC investment proposal 40–1; entrepreneurial environment 25–7; establishing university spin-out or start-up 46–9; first contact with technology transfer manager 40; innovation-friendly and reliable process 39–40; licence agreement between university and industry partners 46; POC as IP commercialisation mechanism at 27–32; POC funding application at 39–40; POC funding by 35–49; POC funding monitoring 45; POC Investment Advisory Board decision 44–6; POC Investment Advisory Board review 43–4;

POC pre-screening routine 41–2; POC project proposal revision before final submission 42–3; review before final submission 41–2; set up of 25; spin-out – commercialisation after POC funding 45–6

University of Oxford University Challenge Seed Fund (UCSF) 4–5; funding success, measuring as function of income 51–3; funding success, measuring as function of project-project connections 53–7

University POC Investment Advisory Board 42

university spin-out or start-up: establishing 46–9; making sure that the project is close enough to the market 47; measuring the market traction 48–9; setting up management team to implement the business plan 47–8

venture capitalists (VCs): and POC 3; and prototyping funding 29–30

"White Paper on the United Kingdom's Competitiveness" 11, 25

Wiesner, Jerome 8

Wilcoxon–Mann–Whitney test 62n1

Wilcoxon rank-sum test 62n1

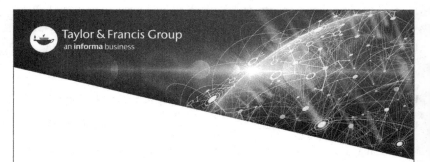